THE OFFICIAL ILLUSTRATED HISTORY

HarperCollins*Publishers*

THE OFFICIAL ILLUSTRATED HISTORY

IAN HARRISON

WITH PAT HAMMOND

HarperCollins*Publishers*

First published in Great Britain in 2002 by

HarperCollins*Publishers*

77–85 Fulham Palace Road

London W6 8JB

This Production 2012

Created, designed and edited by Essential Works

Design: Barbara Saulini

Photography: Colin Bowling

Editorial: Emma Dickens and Dea Brøvig

Printed in China by Shouth China Printing Co, Ltd

A catalogue record for this book is available from the British Library

ISBN 978-000-792138-6

Below Spot the difference – the real SR Class E5 tank and LNER Class N2 tanks did not look so similar as the Dublo versions.

On the face of it, it's a simple story: Frank Hornby invents toy trains, the trains get better and better and, 80-odd years later, at the turn of the new millennium, they are still considered to be the best. But, like most stories, the Hornby tale is not quite that simple. To begin with, perhaps surprisingly in the light of the quasi-generic use of his name in relation to model railways, Frank Hornby *did not* invent the toy train. And secondly, there were two hugely significant interruptions to the development of Hornby trains between the first 'Hornby Clockwork Train' of 1920 and the super-detailed models and the Hornby Virtual Railway of the 21st century.

Toy trains were being manufactured long before the birth of Frank Hornby. The first and the cheapest were trains that could be pushed along or pulled by a string, and clockwork locomotives began to appear in the 1860s (during which decade Frank Hornby was born), along with steam-powered toy trains that were known as 'dribblers' because of the leakage from the boilers and cylinders. Model trains were very different from toy trains (the gap between the two

has closed since), the first models being made by railway engineers in order to test out their ideas and designs before building full-sized locomotives. The tradition of model-making was continued by amateur and professional engineers who would create their own model locomotives from scratch, either recreating in miniature their favourite real locomotives or creating new designs of their own.

There was no set scale or gauge for these toys and models until 1891, when the German company Märklin proposed a standard set of gauges and introduced toy trains of 48 mm gauge which became known as Gauge 1. This was very much larger than the standard size prevalent in Britain today, which measures 16.5 mm between the rails. Märklin later introduced larger gauges known as Gauges 2 and 3, and a smaller gauge known as Gauge 0.

The progression from clockwork and steam to electric power came at the turn of the century, with electric toy railways introduced to the general public at the 1900 Paris Exhibition. This exhibition was attended by W J Bassett-

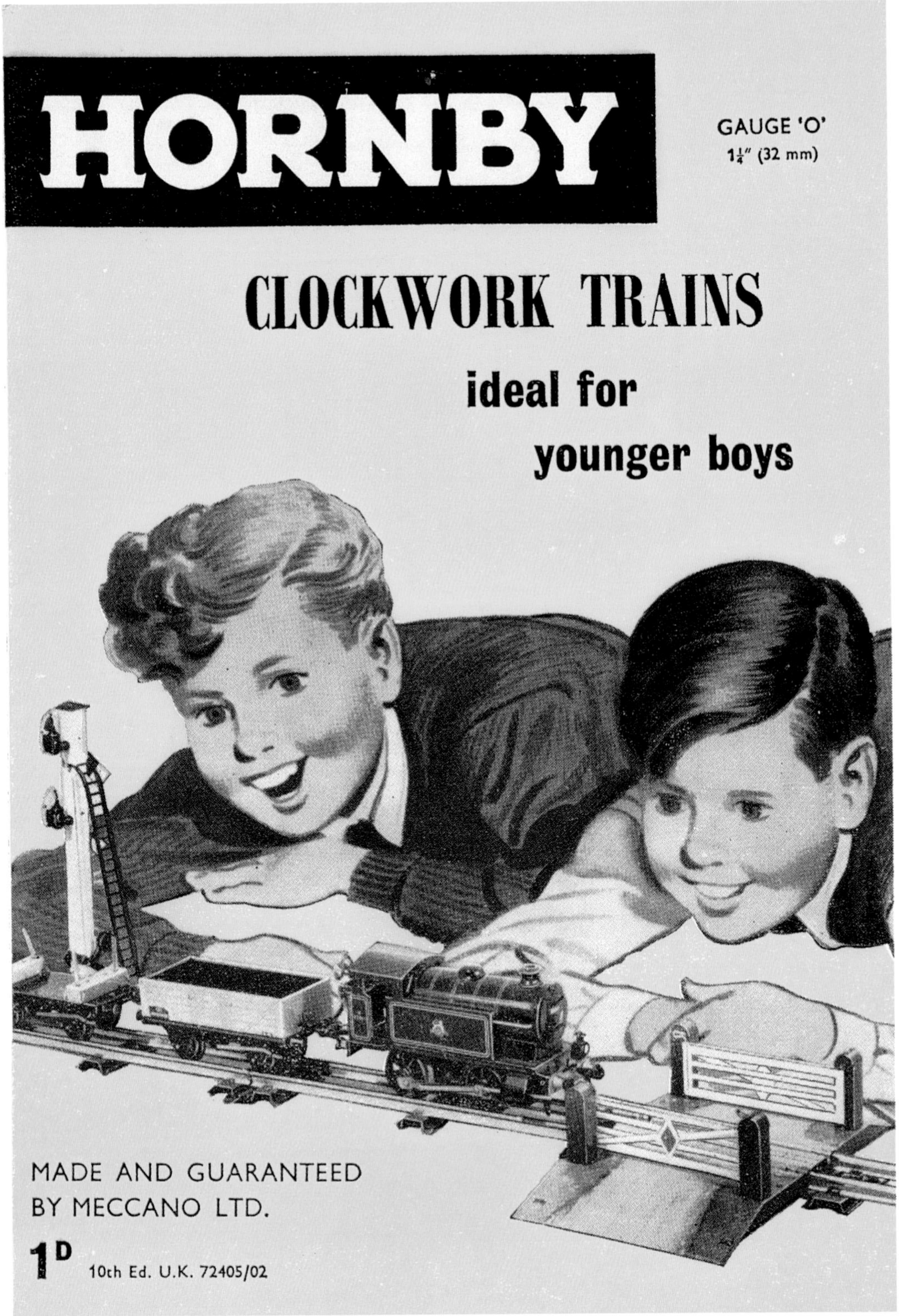

HORNBY
GAUGE 'O'
1¼" (32 mm)
CLOCKWORK TRAINS
ideal for
younger boys
MADE AND GUARANTEED
BY MECCANO LTD.
1D
10th Ed. U.K. 72405/02

Left A 1962 Gauge O brochure.

Above Named after their creator, New York cabinet-maker George Mortimer Pullman, luxury Pullman coaches have always been popular on both real and model railways.

Lowke, 'the father of British toy trains', who was so impressed with the predominantly German-manufactured toy railways that he struck a deal with the manufacturer Bing to produce toy trains based on those of the British railway companies, and began to import them for the British mass market.

So Frank Hornby did not invent the toy train, nor even introduce it to British children. What he did invent was Meccano, one of the most successful constructional toys of all time. As well as Meccano, Frank Hornby clearly had a parallel interest in toy railways, patenting a railway game called Raylo in 1915, and in the same year exhibiting at the British Industries Fair a tinplate model train very similar to the German-designed trains imported by Bassett-Lowke. The breakthrough for Hornby Trains came just after World War II when Frank Hornby introduced an entirely new type of toy train as an extension to the Meccano range, and which was built from components that could be dismantled according to the Meccano principle. The quality of this

train, together with the anti-German sentiment that followed the war, meant that the 'Hornby Clockwork Train', as it was known, made an immediate impact on a market hitherto dominated by German manufacturers.

It soon became clear that this first Hornby train was more than simply an extension of the Meccano range, and that Hornby trains were a resounding success in their own right. A range of Gauge 0 clockwork trains was produced, trackside accessories were introduced, and soon Hornby's clockwork toy train had become part of a complete miniature railway system known as the Hornby Series. Electric trains were introduced in 1925 and the Hornby Series went from strength to strength, continuing its domination of the British market. But by the time Hornby's Gauge 0 system reached the pinnacle of its achievements courtesy of the introduction of the 'Princess Elizabeth' Locomotive in 1937, sales of the Hornby Series were being encroached upon by the even smaller Trix Twin Railway, manufactured and marketed in association with Bassett-Lowke.

The Trix railway was a miniature table-top railway built to Half-0, or H0 gauge. In 1938, one year after the launch of the 'Princess Elizabeth' and two years after the death of Frank Hornby, Meccano launched its own miniature system but of a slightly different size, known as Double-0 or 00 Gauge and marketed by Meccano as Hornby-Dublo. Although the Gauge 0 system continued to be produced at the same time as Dublo, it took a back seat, and the introduction of Dublo proved to be the first of the evolutionary leaps that took Hornby trains from their simple beginnings towards the sophisticated systems of the 21st century. Dublo proved to be an even greater success than Gauge 0, and few argued with Meccano's claim that Hornby-Dublo was 'the finest system in the world for the development of a complete miniature railway where space is limited'.

However, despite the undoubted quality of the Dublo system, Meccano was not quick enough to adapt to changing market conditions during the 1950s, and in 1964 found itself the subject of a take-over by Lines Bros, the parent

company of Meccano's greatest post-war rival Rovex, which was the manufacturer of Tri-ang Railways. The two railway systems were 'amalgamated', but only two former Hornby-Dublo items were truly incorporated into the new range, and in one sense the development of Hornby trains came to an end there. But, just as car marques do not disappear when they are bought by another manufacturer, the famous Hornby name was kept alive in the form of

Above One of the earliest Hornby Gauge 0 locomotives.
Below A selection of Mk 4 coaches, first introduced in 1990.

Tri-ang Hornby, the name given to the new system, and the development of 'Hornby' railways continued along another path. This was not so much an evolutionary leap as a complete change of direction, but once again the name Hornby was attached to the market leader in model railways. With the demise of Lines Bros in 1971, the Tri-ang name was sold as part of the company assets and the railway system became known as Hornby Railways, which managed to retain its position as market leader by producing ever more accurate and detailed trains that by the dawn of the new millennium had virtually closed the gap between 'toys' and 'models'.

Hornby Trains: The Official Illustrated History charts the development of these, the three main railway systems that have borne the Hornby name since the introduction of the first Hornby train in 1920, but confines its remit to those models produced in Britain for the British market. This book does not discuss the models designed and made in the overseas factories of Meccano or Lines Bros, nor the Tri-ang Hornby 'Transcontinental' range which, though available in Britain, was produced primarily for the foreign market. The dates applied to the models can often be misleading, with production of some models being delayed so that they were not available in the year in which they appeared in the price lists or catalogues, others not appearing in catalogues at all, and old stocks of some models being advertised long after production had ceased. Generally speaking, dates referred to in this book as being the date of introduction of a model mean the dates when the model was first mentioned in catalogues or price lists, and dates referred to as being the date of availability mean the dates when the model was actually available in the shops.

As well as being selective in the breadth of its subject matter, this book is also selective rather than comprehensive in its depth of detail. Of necessity this is an overview rather than a fully detailed appraisal of three distinct and complex subjects, each of which has been covered in greater depth by specialist authors. For details of every locomotive and every item of rolling stock, every accessory and every piece of track produced under the Hornby name, readers should consult *The Hornby Gauge 0 System* by Chris and Julie Graebe, *Hornby Dublo Trains* by Michael Foster and *The Story of Rovex* (three volumes) by Pat Hammond.

Rather than trying to describe every element of each system, *Hornby Trains: The Official Illustrated History* tells the overall story of the Hornby name by looking at the most significant developments in each of these model railway systems; those that represented a technical step forward or an aesthetic milestone, or were a reflection of significant changes on Britain's real

Below Hornby-Dublo 'Duchess' class locomotives 'City of London' and 'City of Liverpool' are pictured here with the only known surviving examples of packaging that suffered from a lack of ink during the print run – the result was box illustrations showing the locomotives in the wrong colour.

Opposite page The 1960 brochure.

railway system. This approach produces a slight distortion of the Hornby picture because the significant developments tended to be in the glamorous 'flagship' locomotives at the top of the range. Concentrating on these locomotives sometimes comes at the expense of discussing ongoing improvements to and variations of the middle-of-the-range locomotives or the wagons and rolling stock, the 'bread and butter' of all three systems. However, it is a small price to pay for the descriptions and illustrations of landmark achievements such as the No 2 Specials and the 'Princess Elizabeth' in Gauge 0, the 'Bristol Castle' in Dublo, or Hornby's recent Rebuilt Merchant Navy class locomotive, described by one critic as 'the finest model they have ever designed' – which is saying a lot about a brand which has frequently seen the model railway press reaching for superlatives in the 82 years covering these incarnations of the name.

As well as providing the landmark technical achievements, the glamour locomotives were also the ones that grabbed the headlines, both on the real railways and on the model railways: the Hornby-Dublo 'Cardiff Castle' appearing in the *Guinness Book of Records* for its endurance feat of 153 miles non-stop; the Hornby-Dublo 'Deltic' hauling a 2.5-stone child on a specially constructed 00 Gauge trolley; the model A4s and Princess Coronations recalling the quest for speed, a record that passed between the LMS and the LNER before finally being held for good by Gresley's 'Mallard'; the irony of Hornby's 'tilting train' reaching full production when the real thing did not; and the undeniable romance of the 'Flying Scotsman', produced by Hornby in no less than 18 different versions.

Hornby Trains: The Official Illustrated History is a fascinating journey through the development of what has become a British institution, and it is the first book to treat pre- and post-take-over Hornby as part of the same heritage. Many collectors consider the two to be entirely separate but, for better or worse, for richer or poorer, in sickness and in health, the histories of Tri-ang and Hornby, two of the great brands of model railways, have been inextricably entwined since 1964. Those being introduced to Hornby trains today know only the name Hornby, and for them it is not important whether the trains are direct descendants of Meccano or Rovex. For them Hornby means only one thing: the best in model railways – and of that Frank Hornby would have been proud.

Opposite page A testing time…

The Rise
and Rise
of Gauge O

Below Frank Hornby, central foreground in bow-tie, showing a group of guests round the Meccano factory.

The first Hornby train set appeared in Britain's toyshops during the second half of 1920 at a price of twenty-seven shillings and sixpence. Marketed as 'The Hornby Clockwork Train', it comprised a very basic locomotive and tender in one of three plain colours (red, green or black), a single open truck, and several sections of tinplate track that made up either a circle or an oval. This simple toy train was a far cry from the super-detailed models, accurate railway company liveries and intricate layouts of today's Hornby trains, but it was a significant milestone in a series of developments destined to carry the Hornby name into the 21st century.

The company told its customers that 'We are very proud of this fine clockwork train system, and it will be a great favourite amongst boys', while dealers were informed that 'with the introduction of this line commences a new era in clockwork train construction' – and so it proved to be. But the launch of this first train set was by no means the beginning of the Hornby story. Nineteen years earlier, on 9 January 1901, Liverpool shipping clerk Frank Hornby had been granted a patent for Mechanics Made Easy, the constructional toy that was to make his fortune. Mechanics Made Easy was later renamed Meccano, and it was from the resulting business, incorporated as a joint stock company in June 1908, that Hornby trains derived.

Frank Hornby was the seventh of eight children, and was officially born on 15 May 1863, although it seems that he was actually born on 2 May. His birth certificate registers the date of birth as 15 May but the earlier date is recorded in the family Bible in his mother's handwriting. What *is* known for certain is that he was born at 77 Copperas Hill in Liverpool, a street which now crosses the tracks leading into and out of the city's Lime Street Station – a particularly apt birthplace for the man who was to bring model railways into millions of homes. As he grew up, Frank Hornby nurtured an ambition to be an inventor, and he patented several ideas in his youth, none of which proved to be a commercial success. In a biography originally published by the Meccano Company in 1915, M P Gould describes how Hornby 'thought before he reached the goal that he was beaten, but trying to think of something that would please his own little boys at last showed him the way to realise his ambitions'.

According to what has become the official account, it was while on a train journey from Liverpool to Birmingham one Christmas Eve that Frank Hornby had the sudden inspiration that was to change his life. Gould describes Hornby's journey in great detail and tells how, 'as he rumbled over the bridges, and saw the great derricks and cranes at work in building

operations, and saw the wagons and the various machines and the factories along the way, he began to dream how as a boy he had so wanted to build a bridge, how he had wanted to build a crane which could lift things and swing them round and put them down somewhere else . . .'. Hornby's obituary notice in *The Times* on 22 September 1936 was more succinct: 'the train stopped opposite a goods yard in which was a small crane . . . and the thought came to him there and then, why not make a toy crane for the youngsters out of small strips of steel?'

However, there is another account of the birth of Meccano, quoted by Jim Gamble in his book *Frank Hornby – Notes and Pictures* from an interview with Mr A G Hayward:

I recall that Mr Hornby told me himself that he first conceived the idea of Meccano in the very early part of the century when he was a young married man with two small boys . . . his wife, Clara, had gone out to do the shopping and he was left to do the baby-sitting. It was a miserable wet afternoon and Roland, his eldest son, then about ten years old, had a bad cold and was feeling a bit bored and discontented as children can at that age. The Hornbys could not afford many toys to amuse the children and he got the idea of cutting up an old biscuit tin into strips of various lengths with holes in them, then fastening them together into various constructions using a few nuts and bolts. He found his own two boys liked the idea and so Meccano was born.

Where the various accounts do agree is that Hornby made the first Mechanics Made Easy set himself by hand, and that the dimensions of that first prototype were carried into production. The trade-name Meccano was registered in September 1907, and it was an early example of the company's understanding of marketing and the importance of a name – a toy called Meccano was sure to sell

better than one called Mechanics Made Easy. Some historians suggest that the name was coined by George Jones (who reputedly came up with the name Dublo for Hornby's second range of trains some 30 years later), but Meccano's former advertising manager Harold Owen maintains that it was Frank Hornby himself who distilled the name from the phrase 'make and know'. One of Hornby's own comments mitigates against the idea that Jones invented the name, and demonstrates Hornby's supreme confidence in his invention: 'I decided on the name because it was one that people of every nationality could pronounce.'

Such confidence helped to make Meccano an immediate success, and the company developed rapidly from its small beginnings, outgrowing three premises (James Street, Duke Street and West Derby Road) before moving to the famous Binns Road factory in August 1914. As well as producing Meccano and, later, Dinky Toys, the Binns Road factory was the birthplace of Hornby trains in 1920. The famous Gauge 0 system was produced

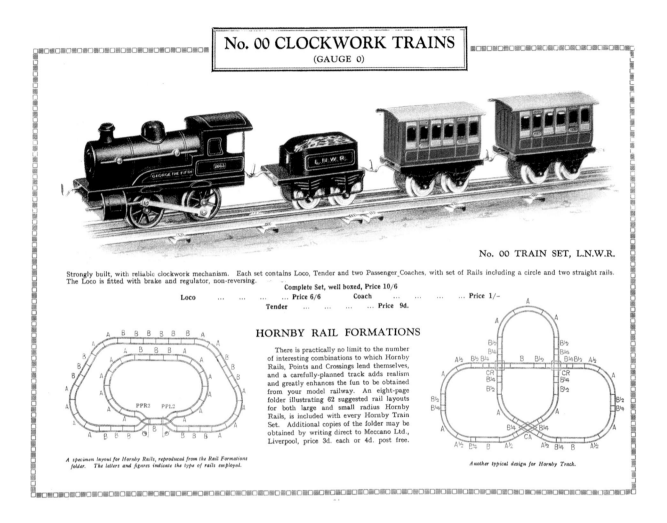

No. 00 CLOCKWORK TRAINS
(GAUGE 0)

No. 00 TRAIN SET, L.N.W.R.

Strongly built, with reliable clockwork mechanism. Each set contains Loco, Tender and two Passenger Coaches, with set of Rails including a circle and two straight rails. The Loco is fitted with brake and regulator, non-reversing.

Complete Set, well boxed, Price 10/6

| Loco | ... | ... | ... Price 6/6 | Coach | ... | ... | ... Price 1/- |
| Tender | ... | ... | ... Price 9d. | | | | |

HORNBY RAIL FORMATIONS

There is practically no limit to the number of interesting combinations to which Hornby Rails, Points and Crossings lend themselves, and a carefully-planned track adds realism and greatly enhances the fun to be obtained from your model railway. An eight-page folder illustrating 62 suggested rail layouts for both large and small radius Hornby Rails, is included with every Hornby Train Set. Additional copies of the folder may be obtained by writing direct to Meccano Ltd., Liverpool, price 3d. each or 4d. post free.

A specimen layout for Hornby Rails, reproduced from the Rail Formations folder. The letters and figures indicate the type of rails employed.

Another typical design for Hornby Track.

there from 1920–64, and Dublo (i.e. 00, or 'Double 0', Gauge) from 1938–64. The manufacture of Meccano and Dinky Toys at Binns Road finally ceased on 30 November 1979.

Soon after the production of Meccano began at Binns Road, much of the factory's machinery was seconded to munitions work for the war effort, although a limited amount of Meccano was still produced on those machines not required by the government. Despite restricted production, in 1915 a toy locomotive appeared in the Meccano catalogue for the first time, as part of a table-top railway game called Raylo. It may seem surprising

that Raylo appeared during this difficult time for production, but in fact the patent application was dated 26 November 1910, and the game had clearly been planned long before the war broke out. Raylo was not marketed under the Hornby name, and the locomotive itself was almost certainly not manufactured by Meccano, so it was therefore not a direct antecedent of Hornby trains, but the introduction of this railway game demonstrated Frank Hornby's growing interest in toy trains.

Raylo was billed by Meccano as 'The Great Railroad Game', and it was described in Frank Hornby's patent application as being 'an intertwined continuous set of rails with sidings normally kept open by spring-controlled points. The points are operated by hand-levers and link-work so that an engine or the like may be kept running continuously round the track'. In other words, players had to operate a number of levers in turn in order to prevent a clockwork locomotive from derailing or running into any of the sidings. The Patent Office requires an 'innovative leap' in order for a patent to be granted, so while Hornby was able to patent the track and the principle of the game as new ideas, he was unable to patent the clockwork locomotive because it was already a well-established toy – and in any case, it is thought not to have been made by Meccano. Circumstantial evidence points to the German company Märklin as the probable manufacturer, in which case the locomotives must have been shipped to Britain before the outbreak of war. Hornby submitted his patent application for Raylo in November 1910 and his specifications were accepted in July 1911, so there would have been plenty of time for him to liaise with his German counterparts in the toy industry before it became unpatriotic to do so.

An article in the June 1915 edition of *Model Engineer* magazine, describing that year's British Industries Fair, reported that Meccano Ltd was 'showing some splendidly finished vertical steam engines and boilers, model clockwork trains, and model saw benches and churns'. The steam engine, circular saw bench and butter churn are well documented (the latter pair were reportedly capable of cutting wood and churning butter respectively), but not so the clockwork trains. No promotional material has yet come to light to suggest that clockwork trains (other than Raylo) were marketed by the company before 1920, but

several workshop drawings dating from 1915 show that a tinprinted train was under development at the time. This development seems to have been dropped soon afterwards, and not picked up for completion until after the war.

The tinprinted train set under consideration in 1915 was a copy of those already being produced by German manufacturers and, although it was produced by Meccano in 1920, it was not part of

the true Hornby pedigree – at least, not according to Frank Hornby's story of the birth of Hornby trains, as reported in the June 1932 edition of *Meccano Magazine*. *MM* stated that a new corner bracket, the architrave (part no. 108), was added to

the Meccano system in 1918, and that the shape of this part gave Frank Hornby the idea of making a Meccano locomotive kit using the new architraves for the cab sides. The Meccano locomotive was made up of standard parts (except for the boiler and chimney, which were specially made), which led to the idea that the company should produce constructional model trains. Thus it became the precursor of the first Hornby train, which was a more sophisticated, though less versatile, version of the Meccano kit. The Hornby Train, launched in 1920, was made up of individual standardised components and was held together with standard Meccano nuts and bolts. Although the Hornby Train was supplied ready-made, it was designed to be taken to pieces and rebuilt in the same way as Meccano. The company cemented the connection with the Meccano tradition by telling dealers that 'boys will look upon the Hornby Trains as Meccano models of a new and delightful type'.

Frank Hornby's ebullience was demonstrated once again in an announcement in *Meccano Magazine* that this would be 'the finest series of clockwork Railway Trains ever made, all designed on a new principle'. Little more than a decade later the Hornby Series would indeed be acknowledged as being the finest on the market. More important was the reference to 'a new principle', because the constructional principle had not been tried before, all the model trains on the market at the time being tinprinted. The revolutionary Hornby Train (packaged as The Hornby Clockwork Train but catalogued as the Hornby Train Set) was advertised as being available in 'one size only, Gauge 0', which was the gauge that had been popularised by British manufacturer and importer Bassett-Lowke before the war. 'Gauge' describes the width of the track, which for Gauge 0 was first standardised at 33 mm and later 32 mm, resulting in locomotives and rolling stock approximately twice the size of that most common today; until 1938 Gauge 0 was to be the standard gauge for the hugely successful Hornby Series of trains, track and accessories. The Gauge 0 track supplied with this first Hornby train set was copied from track made by the German company Bing. The track was flimsy by modern standards and did not even clip together, users being instructed to 'push the rails together with care, and as close up as possible'.

The locomotive and tender of the Hornby Train had nickelled baseplates and the bodies were enamelled in one of three plain colours to represent the London & North-Western Railway (black), Midland Railway (red), or Great Northern Railway (green), just three of the 120 railway companies operating at the time. The locomotives all carried the same running number (2710) on brass plates clipped to the sides of the cab, and the only company crest was Meccano's own trade-mark on the side of the tender: 'M Ld L England' for Meccano Ltd Liverpool, England. Apart from a lack of detail and disproportionately small wheels, the Hornby locomotive looked very smart in its enamelled finish complemented by brass buffers, brass couplings and a brass dome on the boiler. The train was completed by a four-plank open wagon, identical in each set except for plain white pressed-metal letters that were clipped to the sides to identify the railway company, corresponding with the colour of the locomotive: LNWR for the black, MR for the red and GNR for the green.

Why Meccano should have chosen these three railway companies from the 120 available is uncertain: the Great Northern was only the eighth largest of the railway companies in terms of route mileage. It is true that the London & North Western and the Midland were the second and third largest respectively, but the Great Western Railway, not represented by the Hornby trains, outstripped all three of the companies chosen and would have seemed the most obvious choice. But choices are never as simple as they seem to those not directly involved, and Meccano's decision may have been influenced by sales of German-manufactured

Below Tender for one of the earliest Hornby locomotives.

Opposite page Application form to join the Hornby Railway Company, an enthusiast's club run by Meccano for Hornby fans.

trains that were marketed by Bassett-Lowke before the war, which had been available in the liveries of the railway companies represented by the Hornby trains. Bassett-Lowke also produced a model in the livery of the London, Brighton & South Coast Railway, another livery which would later be advertised as part of the Hornby range. Whatever the reason for the choice of colours it is clear that, even at this early stage of Hornby, an attempt was being made to represent some of the actual railway

Opposite page
Top Catalogue illustration of the No 2 Pullman Train, which was first introduced in 1921. Early versions carried Meccano trade-mark transfers on the locomotive and tender.
Bottom Catalogue illustrations of the No 1 Passenger and Goods Trains, showing two versions of the improved No 1 locomotive, with larger wheels and with the anomalous buffers removed.

companies, though without any effort to recreate the liveries with any accuracy.

The same principle of general representation was true of the locomotives, which were a generic 0-4-0 rather than being modelled on any particular type. The figures 0-4-0 describe the arrangement of the wheels in accordance with the Whyte system of wheel notation proposed in 1900 by New York Central Railroad engineer F M Whyte. Under this system the leading wheels, coupled driving wheels and trailing wheels of a locomotive are numbered separately; for the first Hornby locomotive there were no leading wheels, four coupled driving wheels and no trailing wheels, denoted 0-4-0.

At the same time as the Hornby Train Set, Meccano marketed the Tinprinted Train Set which, unlike the revolutionary nut-and-bolt design of the enamelled set, was based on a German design and was constructed and finished using the cheaper method of tinprinting. Under this method flat sheets of tin were printed with the relevant designs for locomotive, tender or coaches, folded into their three-dimensional form and secured to their bases by tabs that were then folded over to hold them in place. The Tinprinted Train Set was advertised as being 'Strongly built, with reliable clockwork mechanism . . . Each set contains Engine, Tender and two Passenger Cars, printed in close imitation of the railway companies' rolling stock'. Ironically, tinprinting, though cheaper and less sturdy than the constructional method, did allow for more (two-dimensional) detail, making the claim of 'close imitation' truer of the tinprinted set than the enamelled version. The railway company liveries (LNWR, MR and GNR) were printed in three colours, with individual numbers on the locomotive (or on the tender in the case of the MR). The

LNWR versions carried the name 'George V' on the splasher, a patriotic detail in a sensitive market just after World War I, and further evidence of Hornby's awareness of the competition – before the war Bing had produced a 'George the Fifth' for Bassett-Lowke, said to be Bing's best-loved British outline model. The greater detailing possible with tinprinting also allowed for railway company lettering on the tender, which, unlike its more expensive counterpart, carried a full load of pressed tinplate coal.

However, despite the greater accuracy of the superficial details, the tender and coaches of the Tinprinted Train Set were not to scale, being far too small, and there were none of the brass fittings that made the enamelled train look so smart. Furthermore, the Hornby Train Set was only five shillings more expensive than the much cheaper-looking Tinprinted Train Set, leading to far greater sales of the former. The enamelled set proved to be a huge success despite its lack of detail, small wheels, and the oddity of having buffers and couplings between locomotive and tender (*not* standard railway practice). Frank Hornby is quoted as saying that 'the success of these first Hornby trains was immediate, and indeed it surpassed all expectations. The reason for this was that the army of Meccano boys had complete faith in anything that was turned out by the Meccano factory, and consequently Hornby trains were purchased without hesitation'.

Frank Hornby was right in saying that his trains had a ready-made fan base, but that was no happy accident – Meccano's publicity and sales infrastructure was second to none, with franchised stores in selected towns and cities as well as regular self-promotion through the *Meccano Magazine*, and

HORNBY CLOCK WORK TRAINS

THE HORNBY TRAINS are manufactured by Meccano Ltd., and they are built on the Meccano principle. All the parts are standardised, and Engines, Tenders, Coaches and Wagons may be taken entirely to pieces and rebuilt. If one of the parts is lost or damaged you can fit a new one yourself. *A Hornby Train lasts for ever!* The Hornby Train is a beautiful piece of workmanship, with perfect clockwork mechanism ensuring smooth running. Each train is guaranteed by Meccano Ltd.

PERFECT MECHANISM   BEAUTIFUL FINISH   STANDARDISED PARTS

The Hornby Clockwork Train No. 2 Pullman

This includes an Engine and Tender of a larger type, measuring 17in. long. A superior mechanism has been adopted making this the most attractive and satisfactory clockwork train yet produced. The Coaches are beautiful both in colouring and finish. Each set includes Engine, Tender, one Pullman and one Dining Coach as illustrated, with set of rails making a 4ft. diameter circle (Gauge 0). In four colours to represent London and North-Western, Midland Great Northern, and Caledonian Railway systems. The Engine is fitted with reversing gear, brakes and governor.   Complete set in gold-embossed box - - price **80**/-

Engines - **40**/- each   Tenders - **5**/- each   Coaches - **16**/- each   (Rails, Points and Crossings see below.)

The Hornby Clockwork Train No. 2 Goods

This is similar to the passenger set No. 2, but two waggons in place of coaches.

Complete set in gold-embossed box - **57/6**

Crossings, right or acute angle - **2**/6 each.   Points, right or left hand (for 2ft. and for 4ft. diam.) - **5**/- each.   Loco. - **40**/- each
Tender - **5**/- each   Wagons - - **4**/6 each   Rails - - **6**/- per doz.

The Hornby Clockwork Train No. 1 Goods

Gauge 0. In four colours to represent the London and North-Western Midland, Great Northern, and Caledonian Railway systems. Each set contains Engine, Tender and one Wagon, with set of rails including a 2ft. diameter circle and two straights. The Engine is fitted with reversing gear, brakes and governor.

Complete Set in strong attractive box - - price **30**/-

Engines -   **18**/6 each   Wagons - - - - **4**/6 each
Tenders - - - **4**/6   (Rails, Points and Crossings see below.)

The Hornby Clockwork Train No. 1 Passenger

Gauge 0. In four colours to represent the London and North-Western, Midland, Great Northern, and Caledonian Railway systems. The Coaches are beautifully enamelled in colours. Each set contains Engine, Tender and two coaches with set of rails including a 2ft. diameter circle and two straights. The Engine is fitted with reversing gears, brakes and governor.

Complete set in gold-embossed box.   Engines - - **18**/6 each   Coaches - - - **6**/6 each
price - - - - - **38**/6   Tenders - - **4**/6 ,,   Rails, straight or curved - **6**/- per doz.
Points, right or left hand (for 2ft. or 4ft. diam.) **5**/- each   Crossings (right or acute angle) **2**/6 each.

this huge marketing machine was already in action promoting Hornby trains as vigorously as it had Meccano. But, apart from a captive audience, a skilled sales team and the undisputed high quality of the Hornby Train Set, there were other reasons for its success: the Hornby Train was launched into the marketplace immediately after World War I at a time when children were very eager for new toys, and it was against a background of anti-German sentiment that Meccano, already hugely successful in its own right, was able to establish a foothold in the toy train market, which before the war had been dominated by German manufacturers. Indeed, *Meccano Magazine* makes it clear that it was Meccano's patriotic duty to supply British-made toy trains: 'For a long time now we have been urged by the Government and by the public to produce clockwork trains to replace those which used to be imported from the continent.'

At the dawn of the 21st century it is easy to underestimate the vehemence of anti-German public

opinion during and after World War I, but a 1916 publication discussing the British Industries Fair (at which Meccano had exhibited Raylo the previous year) makes the situation quite clear: 'Once and for all Germany must be humiliated, crushed, smashed and shattered; and after the Allied armies and navies have accomplished this, the process must be continued and perpetuated by the peaceful pursuit of commerce.'[i]

Having broken into the market at a politically opportune moment, Meccano strove to keep Hornby trains at the fore by virtue of constant developments, improvements and innovations. The years following the launch of the Hornby Train and the Tinprinted Train saw a flurry of new products hit the shelves, and it was quality and innovation rather than patriotic fervour which fuelled the ongoing success of what came to be marketed as the Hornby Series. The March 1921 edition of *Meccano Magazine* promised that 'bigger engines, passenger coaches, new trucks, larger radius lines... will create a sensation in the world of toys next winter'. First came an improved version of the original Hornby Train, renamed the No 1 Hornby Train, with a more powerful clockwork mechanism, larger wheels to replace the rather comically proportioned wheels of the original locomotive, and the removal of the incongruous buffers and couplings between the locomotive and the tender. The No 1 range was expanded by the introduction of a covered goods van to complement the open wagon and, later in the year, passenger coaches in different colours for each of the railway companies, with transfers of the relevant company crest on the sides – the van and the coaches were all built on the constructional principle and had an enamelled finish. The new No

Below Two variations of the No 2 Special Pullman Coach, which was first released in 1928 as the No 2-3 Pullman Coach. Hornby described these as 'the most realistic Gauge 0 Pullman cars that have ever appeared on the market at anything like the price'.

1 Set was also supplied with improved rails that had a greater number of sleepers to improve strength and stability, together with wires to clip the sections of rail together. No longer did users simply have to keep their fingers crossed that the rails would remain together.

A new colour of locomotive and tender was also introduced to the No 1 Series: plain blue for the Caledonian Railway, to pull a CR wagon that had been produced at the end of the previous year. Coaches were supplied to make up a passenger set supposedly in the CR livery, but these were simply the Great Northern coaches with transfers of the CR crest. The Caledonian Railway was established in 1845 and by 1921, when the Gauge 0 model was introduced, it was the seventh largest railway company in terms of route mileage, slightly ahead of the Great Northern. During the war the Caledonian played a significant part in supplying the Grand Fleet at Scapa Flow, accommodating supply and troop trains that were known as 'Jellicoe Specials' after the Commander-in-Chief of the Grand Fleet, Admiral Jellicoe.

For a long time the new No 1 Set also provided modern collectors with an enigma: London, Brighton & South Coast Railway open wagons had been introduced at the end of 1920, at the same time as the CR wagons, and full LBSC Sets were advertised in *Meccano Magazine* (once only) at the same time as the CR Set, but no boxed LBSC Set or locomotive could be discovered. The enigma: was the LBSC Set ever produced and, if so, was the locomotive one of the four known colours or a fifth, hitherto undiscovered, colour? (The actual livery of the LBSC is a yellowy-orange known as 'Marsh umber'.) Sadly, the least interesting explanation was the most plausible: if the set was produced at all, the locomotive probably shared a colour with one of the other liveries. Given that none of the locomotives or tenders carried a company crest and all had the number 2710, an LBSC locomotive and tender separated from their box would in fact be indistinguishable from those of whichever company they shared a colour with. The mystery has now been solved. A No 1 Passenger Set with an LBSC sticker on its box eventually came to light in the late 1990s, providing an answer to the puzzle: the locomotive and tender were in standard LNWR black, and the coaches in standard LNWR livery, but with LBSC transfers on top of the LNWR transfers.

Renaming the Hornby Train Set the No 1 Hornby Train Set was a sure-fire indication that another set was on the way – and it gave a pretty good idea of what the new set would be called. But here Meccano managed to exceed expectations, producing not one but two No 2 Sets: the No 2 Hornby Goods Train Set and its partner the No 2 Hornby Pullman Train Set, consisting of an entirely new 'No 2' locomotive and tender, together with two open goods wagons or two new passenger coaches respectively. At the same time (September 1921), the No 1 Set performed its own bifurcation, becoming the No 1 Hornby Goods Train Set and the No 1 Hornby Passenger Train Set.

The No 2 Sets, like their predecessor, were made up of components that could be dismantled

Above The 'Footbridge No 1 With Detachable Signals' was first introduced in 1924 as a cheaper, non-constructional alternative to the Lattice Girder Bridge.

and rebuilt, continuing the constructional Meccano principle and steering clear of the less successful tinprinting process. The No 2 locomotive and tender had a similar 'look' to their No 1 counterparts, the casings being essentially enlargements of the earlier versions and enamelled in the same four plain colours. The locomotives were again finished with smart brass fittings, including the brass plate clipped to the cab for the running number: 2711 for all liveries where the No 1 locomotives had 2710. But the similarities ended with the casing – the No 2 locomotives had larger wheels, larger motors and a larger 4-4-0 wheelbase (four leading wheels, four coupled driving wheels and no trailing wheels), while the tender was extended to six wheels. The most significant development was that the four leading wheels of the locomotive made it the first bogie locomotive to be manufactured by Meccano. (A bogie is a four- or six-wheeled truck that swivels independently of the locomotive, wagon or coach that it supports.) The extra length of the locomotive and tender made the No 2 Train look a great deal more powerful than the diminutive No 1, and the fact that the large driving wheels of the locomotive actually extended up under the splasher gave the whole thing an altogether more realistic appearance.

The No 2 Goods Train Set was supplied with the same trucks as the No 1 Train Set (although there were two instead of one), but for the No 2 Pullman Train Set there were newly designed bogie passenger coaches. The coaches were supplied in a green and cream livery, and were identical except for their transfers: each Pullman Train Set included one coach labelled 'Pullman' (with Pullman crests) and one labelled 'Dining Saloon', with the crest of the appropriate railway company to correspond with the colour of its locomotive and tender – still a choice of GNR (green), MR (red), CR (blue) or LNWR (black).

Like the locomotives and tenders, the Hornby Pullman cars were not finished accurately in the railway company liveries but were generic Pullmans, conjuring up in the imagination the luxury of the real thing. The name Pullman had been a synonym for luxury on the railways since New York cabinet-maker George Mortimer Pullman introduced the 'Pullman railroad sleeping car', which he patented in 1864–5. Two years later Mortimer formed the Pullman Palace Car Company and in 1880 he founded 'Pullman City' to accommodate workers at the factory (Pullman City subsequently became part of Chicago). The first Pullman cars to be seen in Britain came as the result of an agreement in 1873 between the Pullman Company and the Midland Railway, whereby Pullman supplied, maintained and staffed the cars in return for a 15-year contract allowing Pullman to charge a supplement for passengers using the special service.

This arrangement was so successful that it was repeated with many other railway companies in Britain and Europe, and the name Pullman soon became better known around the world than that of any of the great locomotive designers. Pullman coaches were often referred to as the 'drawing-room car', and one of the early American Pullmans was described as 'a room containing two large and comfortable arm-chairs and a sofa, two broad clear plate-glass windows on each side . . . and mirrors at every corner. Books and photographs lie on the table. Your wife sits at the window sewing, and looking out on long ranges of snow-clad mountains or on boundless ocean-like plains'. Dining cars,

ZULU CLOCK WORK TRAINS

PASSENGER SET

Fine and durable mechanism, and strength of construction in all parts are the main characteristics of this new type of clockwork train. The Zulu Loco is well designed and efficient, and will give long and excellent service. Richly enamelled and highly finished; fitted with brake and governor; non-reversing.

Each set contains Loco, Tender, two Passenger Coaches and set of rails, consisting of two straights, and curves to form a circle of 2 ft. diameter.

Gauge 0, in black only, packed in strong cardboard box .. 25/-

ZULU GOODS SET

The Goods Set is the same as the Passenger Set but contains one Wagon in place of Passenger Coaches.
Gauge 0, in black only, packed in strong cardboard box, 18/6

Zulu Locos each 10/6   Zulu Tenders each 2/6   Zulu Passenger Coaches each 5/-
Zulu Wagons each 3/-

11

Below Among the goods wagons introduced in 1922 were (l-r) the Gunpowder Van, GN brake van and Cement Wagon. The Cement Wagon and the Shell Tank Wagon (not shown) were the first wagons to be manufactured using lugs rather than the traditional nuts and bolts, abandoning Meccano's constructional principle.

which had also made their appearance in Hornby Gauge 0, were introduced to the railways soon after Pullman cars, and were another idea imported to Britain from America – Britain's first regular dining car service was provided by the Great Northern Railway between Leeds and King's Cross, and began in September 1879.

Dining cars came relatively late to the real railways and very early to Hornby, but with other developments the reverse was true: after the dining car Hornby's next major introduction was a footbridge. This may seem like a relatively insignificant feature of a railway but the Lattice Girder Bridge was an important innovation that presaged the next stage of development for the

and initiate a move towards the ever more complex layouts that would ultimately transform model railways from a novelty toy into a creative pastime.

The launch of the No 2 Set was quickly followed by the introduction of a number of new goods wagons, some of them being simple embellishments of the previous covered wagons, while others were entirely new departures, including a bogie Timber Wagon complete with timber (making the coal-less tender look somewhat incongruous) and a Shell Petrol Tank Wagon, the first of a series of tank wagons that would later appear in various slightly modified forms and in the liveries of numerous oil and petrol companies. The Shell Petrol Tank Wagon and a Cement Wagon

Hornby Gauge 0 system. Until November 1921 the various sets had consisted of relatively unrealistic trains running on simple circles or ovals of track. The 'snow-clad mountains and boundless plains' had all been firmly in the imagination, but the introduction of the first trackside accessory, in the form of the Lattice Girder Bridge, was to change all that. The bridge itself was a very simple constructional kit based on the Meccano principle (in fact it was to be Hornby's only constructional item of scenery), but the availability of accessories was to lead to a demand for more realistic models,

introduced at the same time (May 1922) were significant in being the first Hornby wagons not to be held together with nuts and bolts, so marking the beginning of a move away from the first principles of Meccano towards the more modern Gauge 0 system.

While the No 1 and No 2 Sets flourished, the opposite was true of the Tinprinted Set but, ironically, success and relative failure had the same result in the marketplace – a reduction in prices. The huge success of the No 1 and No 2 Sets allowed Meccano to reduce prices because of the

Above The 50-ton Trolley Wagon, with cable drums.

high volume of sales, while the price of the Tinprinted Train Set was reduced by almost half to bargain basement levels because it was not selling at all. The slow sales of the Tinprinted Set were not much lamented, and were in fact a vindication of Meccano's own design and development over the tinprinted principle copied from the German manufacturers. However, Hornby still needed a train set at the lower end of the range, and so Zulu Clockwork Trains were introduced as the cheaper alternative to the Nos 1 and 2 Sets. At first Zulu trains did not carry the Hornby name but were marketed as a separate brand within the Meccano fold, described thus in the Meccano products catalogue: 'Fine and durable mechanism, and strength of construction in all parts are the main characteristics of this new type of clockwork train. The Zulu loco is well-designed and efficient, and will give long and excellent service.'

Zulu trains were stylistically very similar to the No 1 trains, and it was simplicity rather than inferiority which kept the cost (and therefore the price) of the Zulu train low: it was non-constructional, details were kept to a minimum and, like Ford's Model T, it was available in any colour you liked so long as it was black. The clockwork mechanism was simpler, and perhaps the only real disadvantage of the Zulu was that it was non-reversing – though a reversing Zulu Tank Locomotive was added to the series within two months of the first Zulu Train Sets appearing.

Meccano did not repeat its earlier mistake of pricing these bottom-of-the-range sets too close to those at the top and, whereas the Tinprinted Train Set had looked far cheaper than the Hornby Train Set but cost only a little less, the opposite was true of the Zulu Train Set: it looked almost as good but it cost considerably less, at 18/6 for the Zulu Goods Train Set as opposed to 25/6 for the No 1 Goods Train Set.

One of the mysteries about the Zulu is the origin of its name. The explanation in *Meccano Magazine* was that it derived from 'a well-known Great Western train that runs between Paddington and Birkenhead', but the livery of Meccano's Zulu was a representation of the LNWR livery, not that of the GWR. Zulu was not an official name on the GWR but a railwaymen's nickname coined in 1879 at the time of the Zulu War. Being the name of the Paddington–Birkenhead train, perhaps it was the case that someone had seen the Great Western Zulu at Birkenhead, just across the water from the Liverpool factory, and simply liked the name.

The impetus for Hornby's next big development, in 1923, came not from within the company but as a result of upheavals on the national rail network. During the war the government had taken direct control of the railways through the Railway Executive Committee and, by the time the railways were returned to civilian control in 1921, the benefits of unified operations had become obvious. Therefore, rather than returning the network to the control of 120 separate railway companies, the Railways Act of 1921 demanded the amalgamation of these companies into four large groups. The Act came into force on 1 January 1923 in what became known as the Grouping of the Railways, and three new railway companies were formed: the London & North-Eastern Railway (LNER), the London, Midland & Scottish Railway (LMS) and the Southern Railway (SR), while the Great Western Railway (GWR) retained its management structure almost intact and simply absorbed a number of smaller lines.

Meccano responded with the launch of the first Hornby train to be produced in the livery of an actual railway company: the 4-4-4 No 2 Tank Locomotive. For those who were unfamiliar with the use of tank locomotives, only previously available in the Zulu Series, the first *Hornby Book of Trains* issued an explanation: 'As every boy knows, in actual practice tank locos are chiefly used on short runs where smaller quantities of water and coal are necessary for each trip. One of their chief advantages is that they may be run as readily backwards as forwards. This fact enables them to be used independently of turntables, thus effecting great economy in both time and money.' The Hornby No 2 Tank Locomotive, while remaining stylistically in the tradition of the other No 1 and No 2 locomotives, was significant in that it was the first Hornby-branded locomotive to continue the move (begun with the Shell Petrol Tank Wagon and the Cement Wagon) towards non-constructional items, showing that the Zulu-branded locomotives were not simply an aberration in the interests of economy but a step towards the future.

The No 2 Tank Locomotive appeared in the liveries of the London Midland & Scottish Railway and the London & North-Eastern Railway (whose basic colours of red or black for the LMS and green for the LNER were already in production), although these were soon out of date because the liveries of the railway companies themselves were still in flux. Early No 2 Tank Locomotives had the characters 'LM & S' or 'L & NER' on the tank sides, as used by the railway companies for a short while before they removed the ampersand from their lettering, leaving Hornby slightly behind the times. During the same period, the existing No 1 and No 2 locomotives also began to appear in the liveries of the LMS and LNER, but it was 1926 before Hornby sets appeared in the livery of the Great Western Railway, and a further two years before Southern Railway livery would be seen.

Below From 1923 onwards, Hornby Trains began to appear in post-Grouping liveries. Seen here are (top to bottom), a No 2 locomotive and tender (LMS), two No 2 tanks (Great Western and LNER), and a No 1 tank (Southern Railway).

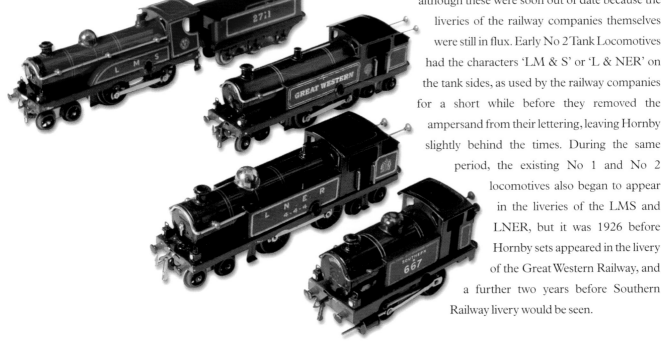

For nearly two years the monotony of those imaginary snow-clad peaks and boundless plains had been broken only by as many Lattice Girder Bridges as a user could buy, but from 1923 onwards new accessories and buildings began to appear thick and fast. Among the first were various lamp standards and signals, a telegraph pole, tunnel, viaduct, level crossing, water tank and signal cabin. There was also a tinplate station, catalogued

simply as 'Railway Station' but with signs at each end of the platform indicating that it was intended, nominally at least, to represent Windsor Station. The following year the station was complemented by luggage, milk cans, benches and even a post-box, but no people. Meccano historian Peter Randall asserts that Windsor Station was chosen 'for obviously patriotic rather than regional reasons', and it is certainly true that, apart from the lack of realism in the model, the name gives rise to two anomalies in terms of realistic railway practice. Firstly, by 1923 there was no Windsor Station: the town of Windsor was (and is) served by two stations, both opened in 1849, and both later renamed 'Windsor & Eton', one in 1903 and the other in 1904. Furthermore, one station was operated by the Great Western and the other by the Southern Railway, neither of which were yet represented by Hornby trains. (The two Windsor stations were renamed again by British Rail in 1949, as Windsor & Eton Riverside and Windsor & Eton Central.)

A large number of goods wagons appeared in 1923 and 1924, including hoppers, tippers, tank wagons, cattle trucks, cranes and even a snow plough complete with rotating fan, as well as a Colman's Mustard Private Owners' Van that has become a prized item for collectors in two spheres – both Hornby trains and Colman's memorabilia. The famous bull's head trade-mark that appears on the side of the van was registered by the Colman brothers in 1855, not for mustard but for a starch used, according to the registration document, for 'laundry and manufacturing purposes'. Colman's advertising was legendary, producing numerous posters, leaflets, mustard pots, mirrors, tins and other memorabilia, and it is interesting to reflect on

Left 1923 saw the introduction of a number of new goods wagons including (from top) the National Benzole Petrol Tank Wagon, which was a variation of the earlier Shell Tank Wagon, the Rotary Tipper and the rare Colman's Mustard Van (a refurbished version is pictured here).

Above In 1924 the Colman's Mustard Van was replaced by four new private owners' wagons in the liveries of three biscuit companies and Seccotine glue.

Hornby Gauge 0 railways were now awash with the names and logos of national companies, displayed on the sides of the new private owners' vans and oil company tank wagons, but 1924 was also an extremely important year for Hornby's own name, for this was the year in which the entire range of trains, track and accessories was branded together under the name 'Hornby Series'. This represented a coming of age for Hornby trains, an acknowledgement that, rather than being 'Meccano models of a new and delightful type' (as they had been described in 1920), the Gauge 0 system was now a successful brand in its own right. The profile of this new identity was raised in 1925 with the publication of the first *Hornby Book of Trains* and the introduction of a sales ploy known as *Hornby Train Week*, during which dealers across the country pulled out all the stops to sell the Hornby brand. The *Hornby Book of Trains* was published during the celebrations for the centenary of the railways, which marked 100 years since the opening of the Stockton & Darlington Railway (the first public railway service), and the book contained a series of articles describing the development of the railways, followed by an illustrated catalogue of the Hornby Series products. The first edition sold out, after which it was decided to publish the book annually, and the *Hornby Book of Trains*, eagerly awaited each year, soon became renowned as 'the finest catalogue in the world'.

why the Colman's van was withdrawn after such a short amount of time: in 1924, after just one year, it was replaced by a number of other private owners' vans in the company colours of Seccotine glue ('sticks everything'), Carr's biscuits, Crawford's biscuits, and Jacob & Co's biscuits (Jacob & Co opened a factory in Liverpool in 1914, the year Meccano moved to Binns Road).

More significant than any of the rebranding, publicity or marketing was the introduction of the Hornby Electric Train Set in 1925, a coming of age in fact as well as name. This was an important development in two ways, for not only was it the first Hornby locomotive to be modelled on a specific 'real-life' locomotive, rather than simply being a generic representation, it was also the first electric Hornby locomotive to go on general sale in England. (An electric version of the No 2 2711 locomotive was sold in France before 1925, and was available in England by special order.) The Hornby Electric Train was modelled on the rolling stock of the Metropolitan Railway, now better known as London Underground's Metropolitan Line, which opened in 1863 as the world's first underground passenger railway. The Metropolitan Line was electrified progressively from 1905 onwards, and in 1925, the year that Hornby's Gauge 0 version was launched, the line reached its northern extreme of Watford. In the same year the Metropolitan Line locomotive, described in the official catalogue as 'the latest type of electric car', was famously shown at the British Empire Exhibition, making it an ideal choice for Hornby's first electric model. The Metropolitan train was a clever choice for Hornby, because the electric models of Hornby's competitors were electric models of steam trains, whereas an electric model of an electric train was sure to win plenty of publicity.

The tinprinted body of the Hornby Electric Train did not have the same charm as Hornby's earlier steam locomotives, but this fact was more than compensated for by the joys of electric operation, which were advertised as 'the latest Hornby thrill'. Unfortunately the thrills were potentially of the physical as well as the emotional variety – the set operated from a high-voltage mains supply connected to three-rail track with the pick-up on the centre rail.

The advertisement claimed that 'any boy can fit up the track and operate the train. It is designed to

run from the ordinary town current of 100 to 240 volts, either alternating or direct. It is connected to the house supply by inserting the adapter, which is included in the set, to the nearest lamp socket. The current is converted to the correct pressure through a 60-watt lamp'. And if parents were not convinced by this, the advertisement reassured them that 'Full instructions accompany each set and there are no difficulties or dangers'. However, not everyone

Below The first electric Hornby locomotive was introduced in 1925, and was based on the locomotives used by the Metropolitan Railway Company between Baker Street and Rickmansworth. It was also Hornby's first representation of an actual locomotive, with the discrepancy between the double bogies of the original and the four wheels of the model largely hidden by the low skirt around the locomotive.

agreed that mains voltage reduced through a lightbulb and a primitive rheostat provided 'no difficulties or dangers', particularly to young boys (or girls) whose concentration was already reduced by the exciting prospect of running their first electric train. It is said that questions were raised in Parliament and that the Home Office insisted upon the withdrawal of the high-voltage Electric Train, after which Hornby introduced a low-voltage accumulator version.

Above A post-war boxed example of the popular M1 Passenger Set. The M1 locomotive was first introduced in 1930.

What fun it is to sit by the regulator and with a touch of the finger send this superb model electric train gliding along the track – to stop it – to start it up gradually – to watch it accelerate!

From the perspective of the 21st century, when we take electricity for granted, this description of what an electric train would do seems to go into an absurd amount of detail. The fact that the Hornby advertisement had to go to such lengths to describe the advantages of electrical operation is a reminder of how rare it was at the time for houses to have electricity, and a measure of just how big a step forward the electric model was from its clockwork predecessors. The fact that it could be stopped at will, instead of only at the brake rail or when the

clockwork wound down; the fact that it could be started again without someone having to get up and wind it: this was a real move towards the creation of an imaginary world in which the owner was in control of his or her trains. It went hand in hand with a big drive towards greater realism, as announced in the September 1925 *Meccano Magazine*: 'Real trains are made of steel and painted in their correct colours – so are Hornby Trains. Real trains pull heavy loads over long distances – so do Hornby Trains. You can build a real railway system in miniature – complete to the smallest detail – if you like. That's why Hornby Trains are such good fun – they're so real that you don't just play at trains – you own and run a real railway.'

Meccano did not rest on its laurels after launching the Hornby Electric Train but almost immediately began to produce new models: 1926 saw a second electric set following hot on the heels of the first, the launch of an entirely new series of locomotives at the bottom of the range, the introduction of the Hornby Control System, and updates to the existing clockwork sets. But before all that, the first development of the year was that the entire existing range became available in the livery of the Great Western Railway, creating a world (or at least a region) of new possibilities for the enthusiast – and at last there were trains that could logically run out of Windsor Station. GWR fans also received an added bonus: whereas the No 1 and No 2 locomotives of the other railway companies were identical in everything but their paintwork, the No 1 and No 2 GWR locomotives were individually tooled with safety-valve covers instead of the domes that were common to the other locomotives. In doing this, Meccano made an inherently unrealistic locomotive look only slightly more like the real thing. It was, however an example of Hornby's drive towards greater realism.

Since the name 'Hornby Series' had been introduced in 1924, the Zulu brand had been gradually absorbed into the range, becoming known first as 'Hornby Series Zulu Locomotives' and then as 'Hornby No 0 Locomotives'. The Zulu had originally been introduced as a bottom-of-the-range set alongside the unsuccessful Tinprinted Train Set and, now that it had been absorbed into the mainstream range, Hornby decided to launch a new bottom-of-the-range set. The M Series Train Sets were aimed at younger users, with the aim of 'catching them early' and instilling brand loyalty to the Hornby name so that children who started with the Hornby M Series would then graduate to the Hornby Series proper. The Series M No 1 Locomotive was supplied with a fixed key, allowing tiny fingers to wind the small clockwork mechanism, and was supplied with one M Pullman Coach as the M1 Passenger Set or with two as the M2 Passenger Set. The entire series was tinprinted, and had more in common with the original Tinprinted Train Set than just its method of construction and its place at the bottom of the range: the Series M No 3 Locomotive supplied with the M3 Goods Set was in fact the obsolescent Tinprinted Locomotive repackaged.

But, repackaged goods or not, the distinctly toy-like M Series did fulfil its purpose of attracting younger users to Hornby and keeping them with Hornby. Bill Mudie, now a senior member of the Classic Train Collectors Inc and a founder member of the Dublo Circle in

Australia, describes how he became hooked on Hornby trains:

I started with an M1 Set just after the Second World War when my father obtained a scarce pre-war set from a dealer in Adelaide, South Australia. The sets, I believe, had been stored for the duration of the war and were released in time for Christmas 1946.

Apparently my father and my godfather had the train out on the living room floor a few nights before Christmas and decided that the circle of track was inadequate, and having thought about the problem for a while, built two long straights made of palings from a fence on which were nailed wooden strips for the train to run along. The device for connecting these rails was, as I remember, quite ingenious, as the train ran smoothly from the Hornby curved rails onto the wooden rails.

Above Hornby's Riviera 'Blue Train' Locomotive nominally represented one of the Nord Railway's 'Super Pacifics' although, as with the Metropolitan Locomotive, it had the wrong number of wheels.

Below Station furniture and luggage, which from 1924 onwards helped add to the realism of Gauge 0 layouts – although it was to be another seven years before any people arrived to carry the luggage, buy the platform tickets or sit on the benches.

Right No 3 locomotives 'Flying Scotsman' and 'Lord Nelson'. The No 3 locomotives, introduced in 1927 and 1928 with one named locomotive for each of the four railway companies, were modified versions of the 'Blue Train' locomotive.

Below The impressive No 2 Signal Gantry was introduced in 1928. The gantry was wide enough to stand astride a double track and supported four signal posts.

It wasn't long before I discovered other boys in the area with Hornby trains and the school holidays were often spent in putting as much track as possible through as many rooms as we were allowed by the parents of whichever house raised the least objection to the activities! Every birthday and at Christmas, my only orders for presents were for books on trains and new additions to my Hornby train set.

Vindication, if any were needed, for the idea of having a cheap Starter Set at the bottom of the range. And while Hornby was successfully repackaging the Tinprinted Locomotive at the bottom of the range, exciting developments were also going on at the top, where the Riviera 'Blue Train' was launched in both clockwork and electric versions (the electric version being powered by a 4-volt accumulator rather than by the potentially lethal mains voltage of the first Metropolitan Train). The 'Blue Train' – a by-word for luxury in the first quarter of the century – was the popular name of the Calais–Mediterranean Express used by the leisured and wealthy to travel to the popular resorts of the French

Riviera. It originated in the Calais–Nice–Rome Express, inaugurated in 1883, but the last leg of the journey to Rome was soon abandoned and the service, now aimed firmly at the British rich, was rerouted to serve the Mediterranean coast of the south of France, advertised as allowing passengers to 'sleep your way from the city's fog to the Riviera sunshine' – if they could afford it. By the 1920s, when Hornby released its Gauge 0 version of the 'Blue Train', the fashionable thing to do was to take the 'Golden Arrow' from London's Victoria Station to Paris, and there connect with the '*Train Bleu*' to take you to the Riviera. However, *Tatler* warned against honeymooning couples visiting the Riviera on the grounds that 'girls who might have caused a sensation at Bournemouth found themselves lost, cancelled out, amid the crowd of bronzed beauties' – Coco Chanel had popularised sunbathing, and for the first time a tan had become more of a mark of status than pale skin. Previously, bronzed skin had implied that one had to work in the sun; now it announced that one had the leisure to laze around in it.

The 'Blue Train' was named not after its locomotive and tender, which were reproduced by Hornby in the brown livery of the French

'Compagnie des Chemins de Fer du Nord' (Company of Iron Roads of the North, or Northern Railway), but after its luxury coaches, which were finished in the royal blue and cream of the 'Compagnie Internationale des Wagons-Lits et Des Grands Express Européens' (*wagons-lits* being sleeping cars). The Hornby 'Blue Train' came with two of these famous blue coaches, one finished as a sleeping car and one as a restaurant car. Producing this train was a clever piece of marketing because the company was not only able to sell the model in France but also in England, where the luxury and romance of the 'Blue Train' were renowned. In England the 'Blue Train' was available only with the brown Nord locomotive, while in France there was a choice of the Nord or the maroon locomotive of the Paris, Lyon & Méditerranée.

The fact that the electric train sets could be started and stopped from the trackside made the clockwork sets appear rather primitive by comparison and in 1926 the Hornby Control System was launched in an attempt to carry the thrill of remote control over to the clockwork sets. The Control System was an adventurous system of levers and wires allowing users to control up to six sets of signals and points using a lever-frame housed in its own signal cabin at the side of the track. Clockwork locomotives that had been fitted for the system could be stopped and reversed or restarted via a Control Rail operated from the signal cabin. Signals and points could also be operated from the signal cabin, but after the débâcle with the high-voltage Electric Train, Meccano's claim that 'the installation of the System is quite a simple matter, no phase of it presenting any difficulty whatsoever' had to be taken with a pinch of salt. The entry in the 1927–8 *Hornby Book of*

Trains maintained that 'the best fun is to be obtained, of course, by placing the frame alongside the Station as in real railway practice. It is then a simple matter to carry out a variety of operations in the most fascinating manner', but the truth of the matter was that the system was too ambitious, and it did not prove to be a great success.

The next big moment for Hornby fans came with the introduction of the No 3 Pullman Train Sets in 1927, again available in clockwork or low-

voltage electric. Despite their grand names and top-of-the-range status, the No 3 locomotives were disappointing in many ways and did not break any new ground in terms of manufacture. Indeed, it is probably true that they raised expectations higher than Hornby could deliver, and *Meccano Magazine*'s boast that they were 'realistic in every detail' was certainly open to question. They were grandly presented as named locomotives in the liveries of the relevant companies: 'Royal Scot' for

Below Two examples of the distinctive No 2 Special Tank Locomotive, first introduced in 1929. The Southern Railway version seen here, dating from 1938, incorporates a bulbholder that was fitted to the smokebox doors of electric models from 1933 onwards.

Above The acclaimed No 2 Specials (l-r): Southern Railway Class L1, LMS Compound, LNER Shire class 'Yorkshire' and GWR County class 'County of Bedford'.

the LMS, 'Flying Scotsman' for the LNER, and 'Caerphilly Castle' for the Great Western. But these were not individual models of the existing trains, rather they were modified versions of the 'Blue Train', all 4-4-2 (where the real locomotives were not) and all identical apart from their liveries, names and numbers (with the exception of the 'Caerphilly Castle', which had a safety-valve cover instead of a dome). It was a good way for Hornby to make further use of the 'Blue Train' tools, but it was not a good way of convincing users that the company was creating greater realism in model railways.

Hornby's No 3 locomotives were nominally based on the Castle, Royal Scot, and A3 class locomotives of the three railway companies. (Southern Railway enthusiasts had to wait until the following year for the arrival of their named No 3 locomotive, the 'Lord Nelson'.) These types had been introduced to the rail network during the 1920s as a result of the companies needing more powerful locomotives in order to pull ever more comfortable (and therefore heavier) rolling stock at ever greater speeds. The necessary

increase in power was achieved by having a greater number of driving wheels, and the success of converting 4-4-0 locomotives (four driving wheels) to 4-6-0 (six driving wheels) led to new 4-6-0 locomotives being built as standard practice. This proved to be a successful move for the railway companies, reducing the need for the double-heading of express trains (i.e. using two locomotives to haul one train), but it meant that even at the most basic level Hornby's No 3 locomotives were not representative of the real thing. Two of the Gauge 0 locomotives had the correct number of wheels but in the wrong arrangement, and in the case of the 'Flying Scotsman', where the real thing was a 4-6-2, even the number of wheels was incorrect.

The Royal Scot class, of which No 6100 'Royal Scot' was the first, was designed for the LMS by the North British Locomotive Company and was introduced in 1927 to answer the problem of hauling ever-heavier trains over the summits of Shap and Beattock on the Euston–Glasgow route. In April 1928 Royal Scot No 6113 'Cameronian' set a world record by making a non-stop run of 401 miles from Euston to Glasgow, and five years later another Royal Scot, carrying the number of the original 'Royal Scot', was exhibited at the Chicago World's Fair and afterwards toured more than 11,000 miles round North America.

The Castle class, represented in Gauge 0 by the 'Caerphilly Castle', was designed by Charles Collett and introduced to the GWR in 1923. It has been described by railway historians as 'one of the most successful locomotives ever built for any railway'[ii] and as 'the handsomest and most efficient express engine to run in Britain'.[iii] Indeed, so successful was the Castle class that the LMS tried to order 50 from the GWR in 1926 but their order was refused, which is presumably what led the LMS to introduce the Royal Scot class a year later. The first of the Castles, No 4073 'Caerphilly Castle', was exhibited as part of the British Empire Exhibition at Wembley in 1924, and No 7013 'Bristol Castle' was later modelled to great acclaim by Hornby in Dublo. ('Bristol Castle' was the first of four Castles to be modelled in Dublo.)

The LNER's 'Flying Scotsman', designed by Sir Nigel Gresley, was without doubt the most famous of the No 3 locomotives but, as with the Royal Scot class, Collett's Castle class played a part in its development. The 'Flying Scotsman' was built as one of Gresley's A1 class locomotives and was displayed alongside the much smaller 'Caerphilly Castle' at the British Empire Exhibition. Much to Gresley's annoyance, the GWR claimed that the Castle was the most powerful locomotive in Britain, and subsequent trials between Gresley's A1 class and Collett's Castle class proved this to be the case. Gresley then improved the design of the valve gear of the A1 to produce the A3 class, which was introduced to the LNER in 1925 and proved to be a huge success. All the existing A1s bar one were converted to A3s by 1948, with the last 27 of the class built as A3s from scratch. Somewhat confusingly, 'Flying Scotsman' was the name of

an express service as well as the name of an individual locomotive, and in 1928 the two names coincided when the first ever non-stop train on the Flying Scotsman route was hauled by the former A1 – now A3 – class locomotive No 4472 'Flying Scotsman'.

During 1928 Meccano finally bowed to public demand and the Southern Railway was represented in the Hornby Series for the first time. The main range of locomotives became available in one of two SR liveries: green with white lining for passenger locomotives, and black with green lining for goods locomotives. The associated SR rolling stock appeared in various new colours where previously the goods wagons of each railway company had been differentiated only by the lettering on the sides of the wagons, so that the SR was suddenly better represented than any of the others. A new No 3 locomotive, No 850 'Lord Nelson', was also introduced to represent the Southern Railway and again, as with the other No 3 locomotives,

Below A selection of milk and petrol/oil tank wagons in the liveries of various private owners.

Above Private owners' wagons provided a good opportunity for adding colour to the Gauge O range, as well as some useful self-publicity.

the 4-4-2 wheel arrangement of Hornby's 'Blue Train' (on which the No 3 locomotives were based) was at odds with the real thing: the Lord Nelson class, which was designed by Richard Maunsell and first built in 1926, was a 4-6-0 like the GWR Castle and the LMS Royal Scot.

These discrepancies may not have been important previously, when locomotives were presented simply as generic types, but now that they were being presented as specific, named models, a greater degree of accuracy was required. This demand led to the production of Hornby's first 'true-to-type' steam locomotives in 1929: the No 2 Specials. With these accurately recreated locomotives and tenders, equipped with new, more powerful clockwork mechanisms, Hornby lived up to its own claim that 'this year Hornby Trains are better than ever'. The No 2 Specials were a huge step towards the quality that was to keep Hornby at the forefront of the market until the beginning of World War II because for the first time, instead of painting the same model in different colours, Hornby tooled separate models

for each class of railway company locomotive represented: the LMS Compound, the Southern L1, the GWR County and the LNER Shire, locomotive types chosen in order to allow as many common components as possible, the main differences between the four models being their individual cabs and tenders.

Hornby's LMS locomotive No 1185 was based on the Compound class 4-4-0 tender locomotive first designed by Samuel Johnson for the Midland Railway and brought into service in 1902. A total of 45 Compound class locomotives were built for the MR and a further 195 were introduced after the MR became part of the LMS in the 1923 Grouping – the Gauge 0 version was based on the later series of Compounds, as modified for the LMS by Sir Henry Fowler. Locomotive No 1185 was built at the Vulcan Foundry in February 1927, two years before the model was introduced to the Hornby Series.

The GWR's County class was described by Derek Cross in *Locomotives Illustrated* as being 'among the least known of the British 4-4-0s'. Designed by George Churchward to follow on from the Great Western's successful City class 4-4-0, the County class was introduced in 1904, so Hornby's choice of model was not quite as up-to-the-minute as the LMS Compound. A total of 40 Churchward Counties were built, including No 3821 'County of Bedford' in 1911, not to be confused with the later Hawksworth 4-6-0 County class introduced to the GWR in 1945.

The Southern Railway's L1 class, represented in the Hornby range by locomotive No A759, was

designed by Richard Maunsell in 1926 as an upgrade of the earlier L class, which had been brought into service in 1914 by Harry Wainwright for the South East & Chatham Railway. A total of 15 L1s were built, having smaller cylinders but a higher working pressure than the original L class. The Hornby model shared several features with the LMS Compound, making some savings on tooling. The most obvious differences (apart from the colour) were the larger cab and the lack of outside cylinders on the L1.

The D49 Shire class, first built in 1927 by Sir Nigel Gresley for the LNER, was represented in the Hornby range by locomotive No 234 'Yorkshire'. LNER later updated the Shire locomotives to the Hunt class, which were so close in form to the earlier Shires that it was relatively easy for Hornby to follow suit in 1935, replacing the 'Yorkshire' with Hunt class locomotive No 201 'Bramham Moor', which took over as the LNER No 2 Special Locomotive.

The launch of the No 2 Specials took Hornby to new levels of realism at the top of the range and, as always, the company was quick to improve and modernise its models lower down the range. These improvements included updates to the No 1 range of locomotives, a shift from 4- to 6-volt operation for electric locomotives across the range, and the introduction of further items of electric track to reflect the growing proportion of electric trains relative to clockwork. New automatic couplings were introduced, and buffer heights were standardised across the entire series at the height of the No 2 Specials. As the M1 locomotives and rolling stock were improved, new bottom-of-the-range items designated M0 were brought out in 1930 to fill the gap at the cheaper end of the scale,

accompanied by an M Series station and accessories. The following year saw a further important addition to the M Series in the shape of the hugely popular M3 Tank Locomotive.

A further significant innovation was the Modelled Miniatures No 1 Station Staff which appeared in 1931. These were the first Hornby-made figures to adorn the Gauge 0 system (previously users had been forced to make do with the lead figures that were on general sale in toyshops), and they were the first of what was destined to become another famous – and successful – Meccano brand: Dinky Toys. The station staff were later followed by farmyard animals, passengers, and engineering, train and hotel staff to populate the Hornby world, which could also now be decorated with

Above Looking very similar to the No 1 Tank Locomotive, the M3 Tank Locomotive was one of the most popular locomotives in the M Series.

Below The Water Tower and No 2 'Windsor' Signal Box, both introduced in 1924. The No 2 Single Arm Signal was first introduced the same year, with the No 2 Double Signal following in 1927: the electric versions seen here (No 2E Single and Double Arm Signals) were both introduced in 1932.

miniature railway posters on scale hoardings. New accessories were continuously being added to the Hornby Series; these included tunnels, cuttings and 'countryside sections' complete with fields, hedges, country lanes and gates.

The most important developments for Meccano during this period went hand in hand with developments in the outside world: electrical technology. More and more houses had access to electricity, leading to a huge increase in the number of electric trains available, and at the same time Meccano was constantly improving its motors and drive mechanisms. While there were very few new locomotives in the six years following the No 2 Specials (most of the 'new' models were improvements on the existing range), there was a huge increase in the number available in electric as well as clockwork versions, which led to a large number of catalogue entries with increasingly confusing code numbers representing different versions of the same model: L for Locomotive,

together with S denoting Special, T for Tank and E for Electric, followed by the original model number and then the voltage, led to models designated LST1/20, LSTM3/20, LE2/20, EM36, E16 or (with a Permanent Magnet motor) EPM16, in a confusing array of types that were essentially variations of the Nos 1, 2 and 3 locomotives or the M Series.

But far more important than the increasing number of electric models available (or their confusing designations) was their increase in efficiency and power. After the potentially dangerous introduction of the high-voltage Metropolitan Train Set in 1925, all further electric models had been low-voltage, operating through an accumulator. At first these had been 4-volt, later increased to 6-volt, and in 1930 Hornby produced a 15-volt No 3 locomotive for sale in Canada in the livery of the Canadian Pacific railway. A year later a 20-volt motor was used in a locomotive for the French market, which proved a success and was used in three locomotives in Britain in 1932. This development also saw the launch of two 20-volt transformers made by Meccano, being more efficient than accumulators and allowing the locomotives to run at variable speeds. The more expensive of the transformers also included an output for powering accessories which were wired

HORNBY TRAINS

BRITISH MADE
AND
GUARANTEED

MANUFACTURED BY MECCANO LIMITED, LIVERPOOL.

for lighting, including engine sheds, signal boxes, signals, platform lighting and warning lights on buffer stops. 1933 saw the introduction of three 6-volt transformers of varying outputs and further additions and improvements to the 20-volt range of transformers, and 1934 saw yet another electrical innovation with Hornby's patented 20-volt automatic reverse mechanism. Despite the enormous advantages of the 20-volt system, 6-volt versions of most locomotives remained available to cater for those who did not yet have mains electricity and still had to use the old 6-volt accumulators.

The 1930s were the 'golden years' of Hornby Gauge 0 trains, and it is often speculated as to what might have happened if World War II had not interrupted production when it did. However, before the world-wide upheavals of the war, the company had its own upheaval to contend with – the death of its founder and leader Frank Hornby on 21 September 1936 at the age of 73. As well as his phenomenal success in the toy industry with Meccano, Hornby Trains and Dinky Toys, Frank Hornby had, at the age of 68, been elected Unionist MP for Everton in October 1931. He retired from Parliament at the following General Election in

Below Seeing double – somewhat unrealistically, even by the standards of the day, two No 2 Specials representing the same locomotive, the No 234 'Yorkshire', wait outside the engine sheds on the cover of a 1932 Meccano publicity booklet.

This page The No 0 series of vans was introduced in 1931 comprising perishable goods vans: seen here is a selection of meat, milk, fish and refrigerator vans.

order to be able to devote more attention to his business but died only a year later, after which his son Roland Hornby took over as chairman, with his other son Douglas on the board of five directors. Frank Hornby's obituary in *The Times* recorded that: 'An indubitably great public benefactor has just passed away in Mr Frank Hornby', while *Meccano Magazine* lamented the loss of a father-figure who was active to the end: 'Frank Hornby's active brain was always searching for new ideas . . . He never lost his enthusiasm and up to the time of his death was full of schemes for new products.'

One of these new products, released in the year that Hornby died, was the No 0 Silver Jubilee

Clockwork Train Set. This set was based on Gresley's streamlined locomotives that had begun the LNER's Silver Jubilee service between King's Cross and Newcastle in September 1935, the year of George V's silver jubilee. The jubilee celebrations had begun with a service in St Paul's on 6 May (the anniversary of the King's accession to the throne) and had continued into the summer, with the King surprised to find how popular he really was: his diary records that there was 'the greatest number of people in the streets that I have ever seen', and he is reported to have said after the thanksgiving service that 'I am beginning to think they must really like me for myself'.

For its part, the LNER joined in the celebrations with its new high-speed Silver Jubilee service, advertised as the fastest in the country – it was scheduled to run at an average speed of 70 mph for the entire journey, but on its press run twice reached a record 112 mph, and regularly completed the London–Newcastle run more than an hour faster than any train before it. This special service was hauled by four of the celebrated A4 class locomotives, 'Silver Link', 'Silver King', 'Quicksilver' and 'Silver Fox', and they proved so successful that a further 31 were later built. Hornby's model was of No 2509 'Silver Link', the locomotive that had made the record-breaking press run, and it looked resplendent in its silver livery and tinprinted detail. Being an M-Series

Frank Hornby and King George V, who died at Sandringham on 20 January 1936, less than a year after his silver jubilee.

Changes in management and in the world order were soon to play their part in a radical change of direction for Hornby trains, but in 1937 the Hornby Series celebrated its glory years with the release of two superb new models that marked the pinnacle of Gauge 0 achievement. One of these was the Southern Railway's Schools class 'Eton' Locomotive. The 'Eton' could have fitted into the No 2 Special 4-4-0 series (Hornby's Hunt class locomotive 'Bramham Moor' had simply replaced the Shire class as the LNER No 2 Special in 1935) but was instead designated a No 4 locomotive because, instead of replacing the existing Southern

model (although it was catalogued as No 0), even the discrepancy in the number of wheels was forgiveable, and this model is described by Chris and Julie Graebe in their book *The Hornby Gauge 0 System* as 'one of the most evocative toys made by Meccano Ltd, representing in miniature (however simply) the most modern railway practice, and at a competitive price of only 7s 6d. Even the youngest enthusiasts were now being offered railway-like toys at pocket-money prices'. High praise indeed for a model that effectively commemorated both

Railway L1, both remained available. Like the L1, the Schools class was designed for the Southern Railway by Richard Maunsell and was rated as one of his great successes – 40 were built from 1930 onwards, including locomotive No 900 'Eton', represented by the Hornby model. The Schools were the heaviest of the British 4-4-0s and were claimed to be the most powerful of their type in Europe. The success of Maunsell's Schools class was said to have surprised even him, being conceived as a compromise specifically to work the

Above The Silver Jubilee Clockwork Train Set was produced in 1936 and based on the streamlined A4 class locomotive 'Silver Link', with its articulated coaches. 'Silver Link' was one of four A4s to haul the LNER's 'Silver Jubilee' express, inaugurated in 1935 to celebrate the silver jubilee of George V.

Above The Southern Railway Schools class locomotive No 900 'Eton'. The real Schools class was built in 1930, too late for it to be represented as a Hornby No 2 Special, and the SR had been represented instead by the L1 class. Hornby produced its version of the Schools class in 1937, using the modified frame and boiler of the No 2 Special 'Bramham Moor', fitted with a newly-designed cab. Instead of replacing the L1 in the No 2 Special range, 'Eton' was designated a No 4 locomotive and became the most popular of Hornby's 4-4-0 locomotives.

Below The pinnacle of Meccano's achievement in Gauge 0 – the LMS 'Princess Elizabeth' in its baize-lined leatherette presentation case.

severe gradients and curves of the Hastings line which were too much for the larger King Arthur class. Nevertheless, having been conceived as a compromise (and having been described as 'three-quarters of a 'Lord Nelson'), the Schools class proved itself exceptionally able.

The real achievement of 1937, though, was the LMS 'Princess Elizabeth' Locomotive, described by Meccano historian Peter Randall as 'the finest [locomotive] ever made by Hornby in 0 gauge'. No 6201 'Princess Elizabeth' was the second of the Princess Royal class to be built for the LMS by Sir

William Arthur Stanier, and Hornby launched the model in time to share the publicity for the real locomotive's famous non-stop runs between Glasgow and Euston. Advertisements strove to associate the model with the achievements of the real 'Princess Elizabeth', picturing the Gauge 0 version above a description of the record-breaking Glasgow–Euston run: 'Four hundred miles non-stop at an average of 70 mph; maximum speeds of 95 mph, Beattock Bank and Shap incline surmounted at 66 mph with a 260 ton load! These remarkable feats were performed by LMS 4-6-2

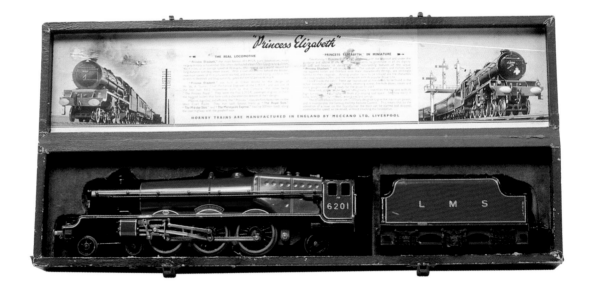

Left 1930s coaches (from top): No 2 LNER Corridor Coach, No 2 SR Passenger Coach, and LNER Saloon (a variation of the re-introduced No 2 Pullman).

'*Princess Elizabeth*' in charge of Driver T J Clarke, on a special run in November 1936.' As well as describing an exciting time for the railways, this is also an example of how the English language has changed since 1937 – today we would hope that Driver T J Clarke was in charge of the train rather than the other way round.

This advertisement also showed a picture of Driver Clarke handing a Hornby Series model of the 'Princess Elizabeth' to a uniformed schoolboy with the caption: 'Driver Clarke says "It's Fine!"' – an early example of celebrity endorsement. But despite all the excitement there was about making railway history, the most significant part of the advertisement in terms of Hornby history is hidden in the description 'LMS 4-6-2 "*Princess Elizabeth*"'. For several years Hornby had maintained that a six-wheel mechanism could not be made, and the technical achievement in finally doing so was enormous. However, it did come at a price – 105 shillings, which necessitated a scheme of deferred payments in order to allow people to pay for it.

Hornby introduced a new set of solid steel rails on a 3-ft radius curve to show off the new locomotive, which suggests that more grand models were intended, but, despite the huge technical and qualitative leap forward represented by the 'Princess Elizabeth', it turned out that 1937 was almost the end of the line for the development of Gauge 0. The impending world war was certainly to play its part but the effects of competition in the marketplace were more immediate. Sales of the Hornby System were being encroached upon by manufacturers producing model railways of approximately half the size, and from 1938 onwards Meccano was to concentrate its efforts on a Hornby miniature railway system that was to prove even more successful than Gauge 0: 'Double 0' Gauge, or Dublo.

i The Next War: The British Industries Fair
ii Observer's Book of Railway Locomotives
iii British Railways' Steam Locomotives

The

Dominance

of Dublo

Never bashful in its advertising, Meccano described its new Hornby-Dublo trains as 'the perfect table railway'. Modern advertising standards would no doubt have compelled the company to say '*probably* the perfect table railway', but this would have made very little difference to the sales figures: Hornby-Dublo was an immediate and unqualified success, due in no small part to the reputation of its predecessor, the Hornby Series.

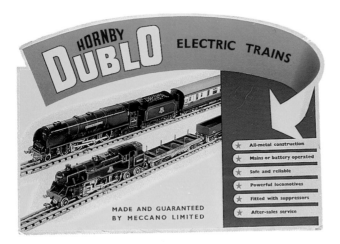

The fact that Dublo was launched just two years after Frank Hornby's death has led to suggestions that he did not really approve of the change, and that his death left the way open for his son Roland, now chairman, to initatiate the new system at the expense of Gauge 0. It is true that the idea of a gauge 00 system had twice been rebuffed in the pages of *Meccano Magazine*: replies to readers' letters in February 1927 and August 1929 stated that 'we do not contemplate the introduction of a gauge 00 miniature railway' and 'we specialize in gauge 0 and do not propose to adopt any other'. However, rather than some sort of conspiracy, it seems more likely that a decade after these letters were written the company was responding to changes in the marketplace, and that Dublo would have been launched with Frank Hornby's blessing had he still been alive. Indeed, a rebuttal in *Meccano Magazine* could almost be taken as a guarantee that it *would* happen: the same magazine had said that there would be 'no great advantage' in changing the Gauge 0 Shire class locomotive to a Hunt just before Hornby did so, and that it was impossible to build a six-wheel drive mechanism for Gauge 0 locomotives, prior to the introduction of a six-wheel drive mechanism for the 'Princess Elizabeth'.

The name Dublo (pronounced 'dubbelow', not 'dew-blow') was coined by the then commercial director George Jones, and phonetically describes the gauge of the new system, '00', or 'Double 0'. Gauge 00 is approximately half the size of Gauge 0, a fact which provides a clue to the changing market demands that led to the introduction of Double 0: miniaturisation was the name of the game. Houses were not actually shrinking, but model railways were now within the financial reach of people who lived in smaller homes than those of the affluent buyers of the early Gauge 0 Sets – and a railway that was small enough to be left permanently set up provided far more pleasure time than one that took hours to assemble and dismantle every time it was used.

The market for a smaller system had already been tested by Meccano's erstwhile competitor in Gauge 0, Bassett-Lowke, who in 1935 imported the Trix Twin Railway from Germany. This was a Half-0, or H0, gauge system, the width between the tracks being 16.5 mm (at the time H0 was introduced, Gauge 0 measured 33 mm, although this standard width was later reduced to 32 mm). Trix also had several revolutionary features, the most significant of which was that trains were powered by the centre rail with either left-hand or right-hand pick-ups, which meant that two trains could be run independently at different speeds on the same track. The Christmas 1935 imports sold so quickly, despite being available only in German liveries, that Bassett-Lowke began manufacturing Trix in Northampton, producing British-liveried models during 1936. Trix proved so popular that it became 'a serious competitor to Hornby',[1] although the very fact that success was measured by its relationship to Hornby's sales is a sign of how dominant the Hornby Series was at the time.

The competition from Trix was serious enough to push Meccano into investigating its own miniature system, but rather than simply copying the gauge and scale of Trix, Meccano adopted the prevailing practice of British railway modellers and produced slightly larger-scale models at the same gauge. This became known as Double 0 Gauge, and was popularised by Hornby's trade-name of Dublo. To understand the full reasoning behind Meccano's decision, which gave rise to an anomaly that has characterised British model railways ever since, it is necessary to understand the difference between gauge and scale. 'Scale' describes the measurements of a model compared with the full-size original, and is often expressed as a ratio: in the case of 00 Gauge, 4 mm on the model represents 1 ft on the original, a ratio of 1:76 (compared with 3.5 mm to 1 ft, or 1:87, for H0). 'Gauge' is the distance between the tracks, and is the same (16.5 mm) for both 00 and H0. This means that all 00 Gauge trains are inherently out of scale because their wheels are slightly closer together than they should be: if the track were made to the same scale as the trains, the gauge would be 18.83 mm. (There is in fact a gauge for the truly conscientious modeller, known as Protofour or Scalefour, which has a scale of 4 mm to 1 ft and the correct gauge of 18.83 mm.)

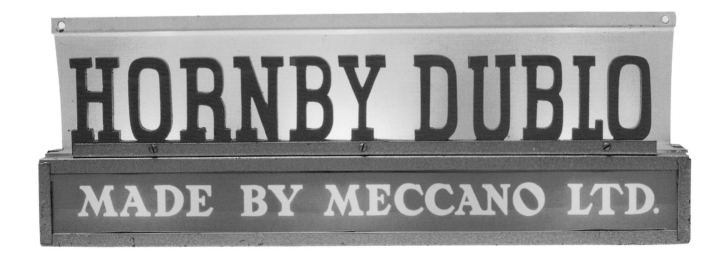

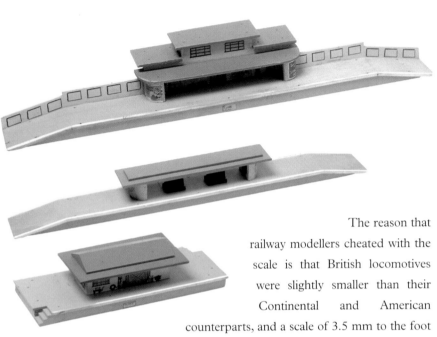

The reason that railway modellers cheated with the scale is that British locomotives were slightly smaller than their Continental and American counterparts, and a scale of 3.5 mm to the foot made it difficult to fit standard motors and parts into the smaller casings of British-outline model locomotives. While modellers increased the scale of their locomotives to solve this problem, they retained the existing gauge in order to avoid creating an entirely new track system – and thus 00 Gauge was born. As a relatively minor specialist gauge, Double 0 would probably not have come to prominence had it not been for Meccano's decision to adopt it, but having done so, Hornby-Dublo dominated the market to such a degree that other manufacturers followed suit, making Double 0 Gauge the norm. As a result, British model railways are still predominantly Double 0, in contrast to American and European model railways which have remained with the 'correct' H0.

Meccano's own publicity leaves no doubt that the purpose of Dublo was to compete in the miniature market, being billed variously as 'the perfect miniature railway', 'the perfect table railway' and, plainer still, 'a complete scale

miniature railway in a small space'. But Dublo was not merely a smaller version of the Gauge 0 system, nor was it a simple copy of existing H0 or 00 systems. As with the launch of Gauge 0 nearly two decades earlier, Meccano brought its expertise to bear and produced a system that represented a significant improvement on those already available.

The Hornby system ran on 12 volts DC, twice the voltage of most other miniature systems and much cheaper and more easily controlled than the Trix 14 volt AC system. Dublo locomotives were die-cast (although rolling stock was still tinplate), and Hornby paid far more attention to the detail of the models than Trix did, having perfected its die-casting techniques in the manufacture of Dinky Toys. The weight of the metal locomotives together with the high quality of the three-rail track (which was also manufactured at Binns Road), meant that Hornby-Dublo quickly built up a reputation for smooth running. But, perhaps most importantly of all, Hornby managed to produce its Dublo system at a fraction of the price of its competitors.

Hornby launched Dublo at a time when Trix already had a full system available, including a range of locomotives, coaches and goods wagons, as well as trackside buildings, figures and accessories. Accordingly, unlike Gauge 0, which evolved over a period of time, Dublo was launched as a full system, 'enabling you to lay out a complete model railway on your dining table' – a remarkable achievement given that Dublo was decided on in 1937 and available in the shops by the end of 1938. Former Meccano Chief Electrical Engineer Ronald Wyborn recalls that 'the Board considered the best way to test the market was to initially introduce a tank loco in all liveries and the LNER passenger loco "Sir Nigel Gresley".[ii] These duly appeared in the first Dublo catalogue, together with coaches, goods wagons, purpose-built brass track, transformers, controllers and accessories including tunnels, stations, signals, staff and passengers, all to scale – a far cry from Gauge 0, where there was a wait of eleven years between production of the first train and the introduction of the first figures.

The streamlined A4 class locomotive 'Sir Nigel Gresley' was the pride of the LNER and immediately became the pride of Dublo, sleek and graceful in its windswept casing and striking blue livery. The A4s had a 4-6-2 wheel arrangement, and in a sense Dublo had picked up where Gauge 0 had left off the year before, launching the new range with a six-wheel drive mechanism. Locomotive No 4498, modelled by Hornby, was named in honour of Herbert Nigel Gresley, who became chief mechanical engineer of the LNER in 1923 and rose to fame as the designer of the record-breaking Silver Jubilee Express in 1935 – he was knighted the following year, during which he also became the president of the Institution of Mechanical Engineers. When the Silver Jubilee Express broke the speed record it was being hauled by another Gresley A4, the 'Silver Link', which was modelled by Hornby as a clockwork Gauge 0 locomotive in 1936. The A4's speed record was subsequently broken by the LMS Princess Coronation class locomotive 'Coronation', but in July 1938 another A4 brought the record back to Gresley and the LNER when 'Mallard' reached 126 mph, setting a world record speed for steam trains that has never been beaten. The timing could not have been better for the launch of Dublo, with the

Above and opposite page The Dublo system was launched complete with a range of wooden buildings.

Below Pre- and post-war examples of the A4 Pacific 'Sir Nigel Gresley', named after its designer. During the war the streamlined valance, or skirt, was removed for ease of maintenance, and other changes included a new number and the introduction of a red nameplate.

Below The key to success – the first two Dublo locomotives to be released were the A4 Pacific (previous page) and an 0-6-2 tank, which was based on the LNER Class N2, seen here in the guise of LMS class 69 locomotive No 6917.

'Sir Nigel Gresley' as its centrepiece, and Michael Foster reports in his history of Hornby-Dublo that 'queues formed in shops as soon as the Dublo quota arrived'.

Hornby's 1939 catalogue entry describes the 'Sir Nigel Gresley' Passenger Train Set as 'a streamlined "Pacific" with an 8-wheeled corridor Tender and a Two-Coach Articulated unit'. Pacific is the name used to describe the 4-6-2 wheel arrangement, but two other seemingly innocuous words in this description are far more important: 'corridor' and 'articulated'. The corridor tender was a Gresley innovation that allowed non-stop journeys between London and Edinburgh. Introduced in 1928, these special tenders incorporated a corridor that allowed access between the locomotive and the carriages, which meant that the crew could be changed without stopping the train.

Articulated coaches were yet another significant innovation of Gresley's, the principle being that two carriages would share a common centre bogie rather than being hauled as independent units, as was usually the case. Gresley pioneered the idea in 1907 after complaints that the existing six-wheeled coaches did not ride well – he mounted two of the existing carriages on three new bogies, creating a 'twin' carriage that was connected by the shared bogie. Apart from being cheaper and lighter because of the reduced number of bogies, the articulated unit was also safer in a collision and provided a more comfortable ride – a very rare win-win-win-win situation. The Dublo Passenger Train Set included a tinplate articulated unit representing the teak finish of the LNER rolling stock, and a single corridor coach was also available separately.

To complement the 'Sir Nigel Gresley' Passenger Set (and to cater for fans of the other railway companies), a Dublo Goods Set was introduced at the same time. This was an 0-6-2 tank locomotive, available in any of the four liveries and hauling three goods wagons, a 12-ton

open goods wagon common to each livery apart from the lettering and colour; a 12-ton covered goods van tinprinted with individual patterns of planking to match railway company vans in use at the time; and one of four individual brake vans specific to each railway company.

The locomotive was based on the LNER's N2 class tank locomotive, and fans of the other railway companies had to make do with an N2 in sheep's clothing. For instance, the model pictured in the first Dublo catalogue was in the green GWR livery and carried the running number 6699, nominally representing not the N2 but the GWR standard 0-6-2 tank locomotive designed by Charles Collett. The tapered boiler and front overhang of Collett's design distinguished it from the Dublo approximation, although this was probably to the aesthetic advantage of the Hornby model – Collett's version has been very politely described as 'not a beautiful locomotive' and as

having 'an unbalanced appearance'. The Southern Railway version of the 0-6-2 tank appeared in olive green SR livery with the number 2594, making it nominally an E5 class tank loco, while the London, Midland & Scottish was in black livery with the number 6917.

The actual LNER N2 tank upon which all of the above were based was another Gresley design, first built for the Great Northern Railway as an improvement on Henry Ivatt's N1 tank locomotive. Gresley's N2 was introduced in November 1920 and 60 were built, proving such a success that a further 47 were built after the Great Northern became part of the LNER in the 1923 Grouping. The Dublo version was in LNER black with the running number 2960 on the tank sides, and post-war the N2 was also produced in the LNER's green livery, this time with the number 9596. After the nationalisation of the railways the N2 remained in service with

British Railways until 1960, renumbered 69XXX, and several variations were later produced by Hornby in the BR black livery.

Above One for the gravy train – the Palethorpe's Sausage Van was one of two private owners' wagons introduced to the Gauge 0 system in 1938.

Unfortunately for the realism of Dublo railways, which initially presented the N2 as a goods locomotive, the LNER N2 was built as a suburban passenger locomotive and was most often seen running passenger trains into and out of King's Cross, although this discrepancy was later corrected when BR-liveried N2s became part of Passenger Train Set EDP10.

As with the carriages supplied in the Passenger Set, the wagons of the Goods Set were available separately, giving a choice of five locomotives, twelve goods wagons and two carriages in the inaugural Dublo catalogue. All five locomotives were available in clockwork as well as electric versions, which was surprising at a time when mains electricity was becoming the norm rather than the exception – a point borne out by the sales figures, which soon showed that there was no longer a significant market for clockwork trains. The clockwork tank locomotive was withdrawn before the war, and the clockwork A4 never reappeared afterwards. The electric versions were a huge success – and just in case anyone was in any doubt about exactly how successful, the 1939–40 *Hornby Book of Trains* introduced the Dublo section by saying that 'the remarkable success of the Hornby-Dublo Railway introduced last year has proved our claim that this is the finest system in the world for the development of a complete miniature railway where space is limited'.

Hornby did stop short of calling Dublo the finest system in the world full stop, possibly because Dublo still constituted a small section in a catalogue dominated (in choice at least) by Gauge 0, which presumably the company considered to be the finest system in the world for the development of a complete miniature railway where space was *not* limited. But with the large amount of effort and resources put into the launch of Dublo, Gauge 0 had been almost forgotten as far as new products were concerned, the small number of new introductions in 1938 being limited to two new private owners' wagons (a Palethorpe's Sausage Van and a Power Ethyl Tank Wagon), a few accessories and a 20-volt version of the Metropolitan Locomotive and Train Set.

It has been argued that it was World War II that caused the decline of Gauge 0, because the level

of quality new products seemingly promised by the introduction of the 'Princess Elizabeth' in 1937 was not continued after the war. But in fact it was clear well before the outbreak of hostilities that production of Gauge 0 was slowing down: 1938 may have seen very few additions to the Gauge 0 system but 1939 actually saw a reduction in the range, with no new additions and several deletions from the catalogue. It is certainly true that the war hastened the demise of Gauge 0: as in World War I, most of the factory's resources and staff were turned to the war effort, and when peace returned much of the Gauge 0 Hornby Series did not reappear in the catalogue. But it was already evident before the war that the future of Hornby Trains lay with Dublo, and, from the very inception of the new range, Gauge 0 took a back seat.

This point becomes obvious from a look at the list of new products for 1939–40: while there were no new additions to the Gauge 0 System, the Dublo range continued to expand, with new tank wagons (Royal Daylight, Esso and Power Ethyl, which was also available in Gauge 0), coal wagons, meat and fish vans, cattle trucks, horse

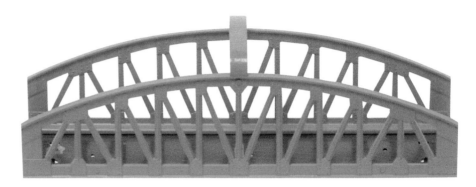

boxes and more station buildings. The 1939–40 *Hornby Book of Trains* also announced the introduction of an important new development in the control of the new model railway system: 'The great new feature of the Hornby-Dublo system this year is the introduction of the Isolating Rail for dividing a layout into separate sections . . . By means of these rails, and special Switches (D2), endless fun can be had by controlling two or more trains independently at the same time. All kinds of shunting operations can be carried out, every movement being made as on real railways.' But perhaps the most significant items in the 1939–40 catalogue were the ones that did not appear in the shops: notably the Duchess of Atholl locomotive and LMS coaches, which were advertised but

This page and opposite page (bottom)
After World War II wood was scarce, and Meccano introduced a new range of die-cast aluminium buildings and accessories of modern design. These included the footbridge, girder bridge, signal box and level crossing.

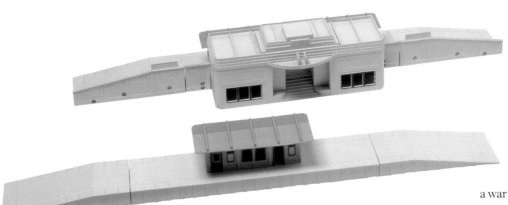

Above The main line station and island platform – further examples of post-war aluminium buildings.

A Meccano trade bulletin for 1940 told dealers that 'One of the most difficult problems in the toy trade at the moment is that of forecasting what is going to happen next season . . . Our Government have told us that they are preparing for a war of at least three years' duration; and they warn us not to indulge in easy optimism, but to brace ourselves for the grim struggle ahead. It seems pretty certain that the war will last at least until 1941.' With hindsight the last sentence looks like a clear case of indulgence in easy optimism, but at the time even a war of only two years' duration must have seemed like a grim prospect. Meccano declared that it would 'go on manufacturing as long as possible' but prices increased rapidly from the onset of war as production slowed down and raw materials became increasingly scarce. The production of metal toys was prohibited by government order from 1 January 1942, and shops continued to sell existing stocks at ever higher prices until 30 September 1943 when the sale of all metal models and toys, whether second-hand or new, was banned altogether.

which did not become available until after the war was over.

On 1 September 1939 Germany invaded Poland. Two days later Britain and France declared war on Germany and World War II began. Once again the Hornby factory, machinery and personnel concentrated their efforts on the war, and production of both Gauge 0 and Dublo began to slow. Some Dublo items produced before the war appeared in the shops after the outbreak of hostilities, and one new item was added to the Gauge 0 range in October 1940 – the grey Pool Petrol Tanker, which reflected the real world in that Pool petrol was the result of the government's compulsory pooling of all petrol supplies. Hornby even made a virtue of the hostilities by advertising Dublo as 'the ideal blackout hobby for boys and their fathers'.

In December 1944 the *Liverpool Evening Express* reported on 'How Meccano Went to War', describing the changes war had wrought at the Binns Road Factory:

Before total war swept across the globe, bringing its toy famine, the fascinating products of Meccano Limited went abroad to every land ...

Today the toy makers are at war. The engineering shops of Meccano Limited, at Liverpool, are turning out not scale models of railway locomotives, or cranes, but integral parts of the engines of war.

Youths who played only a few years ago with Hornby trains and model 'planes are now using weapons and flying war 'planes which depend for their efficiency on products from that same works which produced their toys.

Meccano's legendary self-sufficiency and precision in making toys not only meant that Binns Road became the perfect example to other war workers, it also demonstrated why Meccano's products had been so successful in the marketplace. The *Liverpool Evening Express* article went on to say that 'Their toys had always been engineering jobs. Their world-famous model engines and trains were the products of precision

... their workers had the necessary skills to turn their labours to the new type of work ... This is one of the few works in the country where complete fuses can be made, from the first die-casting to the final inspection. Most other workshops have to depend on someone else for some part or another.' Even allowing for morale-boosting hype from a local newspaper, this is high praise indeed for the quality of Meccano and Hornby Trains.

In his book *Toy Trains*, toy historian David Salisbury laments the fact that 'by the end of 1942 stocks were exhausted and the great days of Hornby Gauge 0 were over for ever, though it did not seem so at the time'. It may not have seemed so in 1942, or even as the war drew to a close, when *Meccano Magazine* announced: 'We are sorry that we cannot supply these famous toys today but they will be ready for you again after the war. Look out for the good times coming!' But it was not long after the war before it became evident that Gauge 0 would not be revived to pre-war levels. Many items, including the prestigious 'Princess Elizabeth', did not reappear after the war, and some that did reappear were deleted

Above and opposite page (bottom) A selection of the first range of Dublo tinplate coaches and restaurant cars, which were gradually replaced from 1960 by the new, more detailed and more accurately scaled Super-Detail coaches.

from the catalogue soon afterwards. Interestingly, the first items to receive an overhaul and reappear in the toyshops were the bottom-of-the-range M0 and M1 Goods and Passenger Sets, suggesting that Meccano considered that the pre-war buyers of the top-of-the-range sets would now be more interested in Dublo, while Gauge 0 should be marketed as a toy for younger children. Indeed, Gauge 0 was in a sense a victim of its own success because, having created a market for 'a real railway system in miniature – complete to the smallest detail' (to quote Hornby's Gauge 0 publicity), it was found that Dublo was more suited to this purpose than Gauge 0.

The 'new' No 101 Gauge 0 Tank Locomotive that followed the updated M Series Sets was a modified version of the pre-war M3 rather than a genuinely new introduction, and the first significant post-war alteration to the Gauge 0 range was the introduction of plastic wheels in 1951. These were introduced because of a renewed shortage of metal caused by the Korean War but, despite being introduced out of necessity rather than by choice or design, proved to be smoother-running and quieter than even the top-of-the-range pre-war die-cast wheels, and a great improvement on the standard tinplate wheels. The next big change was also the result of changes in the world at large: Britain's railways had been nationalised in 1948, and in 1954 Hornby began the changeover of Gauge 0 locomotives and rolling stock to British Rail livery, a much slower response than the change to post-Grouping liveries in 1923.

In 1956 the first completely redesigned post-war Gauge 0 vehicles were introduced, the No 30 Series locomotive, goods wagons and coaches which replaced the M1 Series. These were followed in 1957 by the detailed, tinprinted No 50 Series of goods wagons, but despite these few new additions it is clear that Gauge 0 had been moribund from the end of the war. There were to be no new Gauge 0 products after 1957 and, after a post-war peak in production in 1949, deletions continued to outnumber additions to the catalogue. Gauge 0 continued to languish in the shadow of Dublo until production ceased altogether circa 1963 – there is no record of the exact date of cessation of production of Guage O, but it is known that Gauge 0 trains were no longer being produced by the time Meccano Ltd was taken over by Lines Bros in 1964.

It is ironic that while the political situation after World War I provided the ideal circumstances for the launch of Gauge 0, World War II should have hastened its demise. And the effect of the war on Hornby Trains was not limited to Gauge 0: the war also broke the momentum of Dublo, which had been launched on the crest of a wave of enthusiasm for the well-chosen Gresley A4 Pacific, reflecting the 'streamlined era' of the 1930s and the quest for speed on the railways. In the short time between its introduction and the outbreak of war Dublo had dominated the market, but, although this dominance was to continue immediately after the war, there were now new competitors in their infancy – one of which was to have a devastating effect on Meccano and Hornby. However, until these new competiors found their feet, Trix was still Hornby's main rival. Theatre director Max Stafford-Clark, whose Dublo collection began with the 0-6-2 Tank Goods Set in Southern Railway livery, remembers the situation in 1950:

'It was either Hornby or Trix. It was a bit like living in north London and you either support Tottenham or Arsenal. There were certainly people at school who supported Trix but I was always for Hornby-Dublo.'

But competition was the last thing on the minds of Meccano's directors as the machinery slowly geared back up for the production of Dublo after the war. They were concentrating on picking up where they had left off, with the launch of the 'Duchess of Atholl', the new locomotive that had been promised in catalogues before the war. Peace in Europe came on 8 May 1945 but return to normality was to be a long, slow process.

The July 1945 *Meccano Magazine* announced that 'VE Day has brought nearer the time when we will be able to bring you these famous toys. Our works, which are still on war production, will change over to our own goods as rapidly as conditions permit – soon, we hope!' But it was the same story four months later in November 1945, and production did not actually begin again until 1946, with a limited amount of Gauge 0. It was the end of 1947 before the reintroduction of Dublo was announced, and even later before it was readily available. The December 1947 *Meccano Magazine* carried an advertisement on the back cover announcing that 'Hornby-Dublo Electric Trains are here again!', but this was slightly overstating the case – the details of the advertisement said that 'small supplies of these long-awaited trains are now becoming available . . . the Tank Goods Set will be ready this month. The LMS "Duchess of Atholl" Set and the LNER "Sir Nigel Gresley" Set will follow early in the New Year'. Nine years after it had first been announced in the catalogue the Duchess of Atholl finally arrived and, as with the original launch of Dublo, queues once again formed in the toyshops.

The Hornby-Dublo 'Duchess of Atholl' was modelled on the LMS Princess Coronation class locomotive (also known as the Duchess class) which, during the 1930s, had competed with the LNER's A4 class for title of fastest steam locomotive. The production of the Princess Coronations came as a direct result of the success of the A4: in 1935 Gresley's A4 'Silver Link' set a record of 112 mph which the LMS was anxious to better, so William Stanier, the LMS's chief mechanical engineer, enlarged his existing 4-6-2 Princess Royal class to create the Princess Coronation class. In 1937, locomotive No 6220 'Coronation' (named for the coronation of George VI in May of that year) set a new British record of 114 mph. This record was beaten the following year by another Gresley A4, 'Mallard', making the Princess Coronation class 'Duchess of Atholl' the perfect choice to follow the highly celebrated 'Sir Nigel Gresley' in Hornby's Dublo Series.

Unfortunately for Hornby, though, the 'Duchess of Atholl' had undergone modifications during and immediately after the war, which meant that the company's pre-war catalogue illustrations, and its tooling for post-war production, were now out of date. A total of 38 Princess Coronations were built by the LMS, and for some reason No 6234, 'Duchess of Abercorn',

Below Late arrival – the 'Duchess of Atholl' may have arrived nine years late but the outbreak of World War II was a better excuse than leaves on the line.

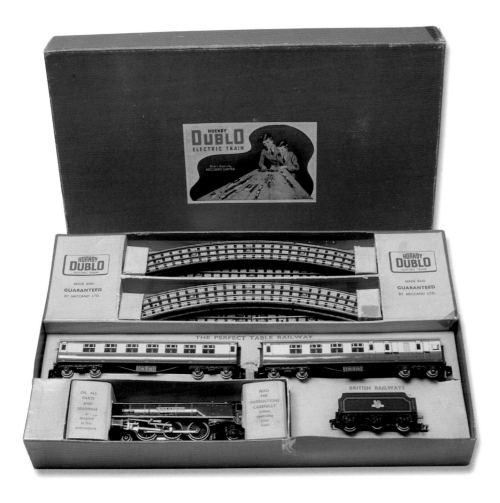

was fitted with a double chimney. This arrangement proved so successful that all subsequent Princess Coronations were built with the double chimney, and the previous models were retro-fitted at the earliest opportunity – 'Duchess of Atholl' was fitted with its double chimney on 1 June 1940, shortly after the Hornby model would have been in the shops, had it not been for the war. The other change was that it became standard LMS practice to remove the streamlined casings of the earlier locomotives and to fit smoke deflectors. (Smoke deflectors are the

additional side panels at the front of a locomotive that look like the blinkers of a horse.) The LMS 'Duchess of Atholl' was fitted with smoke deflectors in September 1946, but the Hornby drawings were not amended to this effect until 1949, so that in the end the Dublo 'Duchess of Atholl' reached the shops with its double chimney and the promised LMS coaches but without the smoke deflectors. The Dublo 'Sir Nigel Gresley' also underwent modifications in order to bring it into line with wartime changes to the LNER version, including renumbering and the removal

of the streamlined valance (or skirt) half covering the wheels.

The arrival of the 'Duchess of Atholl' and the modified 'Sir Nigel Gresley' in 1947–8 was something of a false dawn for the post-war reintroduction of Dublo, because it was to be six years before the introduction of the next new locomotive, which did not appear until 1954. This long gap was due in no small part to the Korean War, which began in 1950: the war not only caused further scarcity of manufacturing materials, but even threatened to place the Meccano factory back on a war footing. Fortunately this did not happen and, although there was a delay in the introduction of a new locomotive, Dublo was making developments on other fronts. These included the reintroduction of passenger and station staff figures (in both 0 and 00 Gauges), as well as electrically operated points and various accessories, while technical improvements included the new Peco-type coupling system and improved interference suppression. What had been sufficient to prevent

electric motors causing interference with domestic radio signals before World War II could not prevent interference with televisions, which became increasingly prevalent afterwards.

Another effect of the war was the nationalisation of the railways, something that had been a Labour party commitment since 1908 and had almost come into effect in the aftermath of World War I. On that occasion the compromise reached by the 1921 Railways Act had been the Grouping of the Railways, but the Labour majority of July 1945 saw the concept of nationalisation become a reality. The Transport Act of 1947 came into effect on 1 January 1948, heralding the formation of British Railways, and it is said that at midnight on 31 December 1947 the drivers of night trains sounded their whistles in celebration. Hornby did not respond as quickly to nationalisation and the consequent livery changes as it had done to the Grouping almost a quarter of a century earlier, and it was 1953 before the first Dublo models appeared in British Railways livery (Gauge 0 had to wait a year longer still).

Below A Hornby-Dublo train set produced just before the start of World War II.

Opposite page The 'Duchess of Montrose' on the cover of the 1958 catalogue.

The year 1953 was a turning point both for Britain in general and for the production of Dublo in particular. It seemed as if a corner had been turned, and that post-war recovery was truly under way – the Korean War ended in July, giving a further boost to public morale, which was already riding high after the coronation of Elizabeth II in June. And for Hornby-Dublo, 1953 saw the launch of three new locomotives with their associated coaches and goods wagons (all in BR livery), the reappearance of large radius curved rails in the catalogue, and the introduction of new accessories including signals, points and level crossings. The only sad point for the model railway world was the death of Frank Hornby's former competitor, 'the father of commercial model railways in this country',[iii] W J Bassett-Lowke.

One of the first new Dublo models to appear in BR livery was the London Midland Region (formerly LMS) locomotive 'Duchess of Montrose', announced in April 1953. The 'Duchess of Montrose' was another Princess Coronation class locomotive, and appeared as a BR-liveried version of the 'Duchess of Atholl' in the new gloss green BR livery lined out in black

and orange, with the British Rail lion-and-wheel logo on the tender. The 'Duchess of Montrose' also followed the new BR system of numbering which added 40,000 or 50,000 to the running numbers of former LMS locomotives, effectively placing a '4' in front of the Princess Coronation class's previous 62XX, making the 'Duchess of Montrose' No 46232. The Hornby-Dublo 'Duchess of Montrose' Set was supplied with new D12 coaches, which were similar to the previous LMS coaches in all but colour.

At the same time as the 'Duchess of Montrose', Hornby launched the A4 class 'Silver King' (formerly of the LNER, by then BR's Eastern Region), also in the new gloss green livery. 'Silver King' was one of the initial group of four A4 Pacifics that had become famous for hauling the 'Silver Jubilee' Express. Enthusiasts had waited five years for a new locomotive, and then three came along (almost) at once – June 1953 saw the introduction of the 0-6-2 N2 Tank Locomotive in gloss black BR livery with red lining. (BR adopted three liveries – green with black and orange lining for passenger express locomotives; black with red, cream and grey lining for other passenger and

Below All three versions of the Hornby-Dublo Class 4 standard tank locomotive, first introduced in 1954 as 80054. A two-rail version, (80033), appeared in 1959 with the new BR logo, and an updated three-rail version (80059) arrived in 1961. 80059 was produced in relatively small numbers and is therefore a rare model prized by collectors.

Left The acclaimed Hornby-Dublo Castle class locomotive, introduced in 1957 as 'Bristol Castle', with the two-rail 'Cardiff Castle' appearing in 1960.

mixed traffic locomotives; and unlined black for shunting and freight locomotives.)

In the spring of 1953 the catalogue number of the 0-6-2 Tank Goods Train Set was changed to EDG17, and it was this set that saw Bill Mudie, a founder member of the Dublo Circle in Australia, graduate to Dublo from his Gauge 0 M1 Passenger Set:

My 0 gauge set grew until about 1952 when we moved house and I found that the boy next door had a Hornby-Dublo LMS Goods Set with extra wagons and a set of points which had a buffer stop at the end. I was absolutely hooked! They looked so real! I had to have a Hornby-Dublo train. I lobbied my parents vigorously for some time until, in the end, I received a Hornby-Dublo British Rail set EDG17 for Christmas 1953. That was the start of a disease which has been with me ever since. I have played with them, collected them, modified them, repaired them and had a wonderful life with my Hornby-Dublo which is now housed in a large, well-lined shed eight metres by five, with a three-rail mainly tinplate-era layout which runs to a timetable, using some fifteen locomotives, sixty passenger coaches and three hundred goods wagons.

The adoption of British Railways liveries was an important and exciting step forward for Dublo enthusiasts, but in effect the three BR-liveried locomotives were simply modifications of the existing stable of A4, Princess Coronation and N2 Tank. However, Hornby kept up the momentum of change the following year with the introduction of an entirely new model, the hugely successful Class 4 Tank Locomotive. Introduced to the fledgling British Rail in 1951, this graceful 2-6-4 tank locomotive, designed by Robert Riddles (who spent four years as William Stanier's assistant), was a direct descendant of Stanier and Fairburn's Class 4-MT tanks for the LMS. Fifty-four Class 4s were built initially, with a further 63 to follow, and the type was allocated to all of the British Rail regions, making it a perfect choice for Hornby to model. Standardisation of design on the national railway system, and the distribution of the type over the entire network, meant that for the first time Hornby could cater for all its enthusiasts

Below Hooked on Hornby – the magnificent red breakdown crane, introduced in 1959, was fully operational, with the jib capable of lifting a load and rotating through 360°. The Travelling Post Office mail van was also a working model, and could pick up and set down miniature mailbags just like the real thing – the TPO even included a hut for the Dublo duty postman to shelter in while the exchange took place.

with a single model instead of four variations. Added to this was the fact that the Class 4 was a mixed traffic tank and could therefore logically be used to pull coaches or goods wagons – and two new goods wagons were introduced in 1954 as well as the promised D13 suburban coaches. The Dublo version of the Class 4 Tank was numbered 80054, with a two-rail version numbered 80033 appearing in 1959 and a modified three-rail version, 80059, in 1961.

Meccano continued to make technical improvements to the Dublo range, including improved power units and the introduction of a battery controller, but the next significant change to the rolling stock followed BR's adoption of a new badge and new coach liveries. To replace the so-called 'lion-and-wheel' badge, BR commissioned heraldic expert Dr C A H Franklyn to design a new badge, the 'lion and crown', or totem motif. Franklyn's design depicted a lion holding a locomotive wheel between its front paws and emerging from a crown that incorporated the rose of England, the thistle of Scotland and the leek of Wales.

The new badge immediately rendered Hornby's existing BR liveries obsolete, necessitating updates across the range. Hornby acted so quickly that history was to repeat itself in that the Dublo models were to follow a pattern set by the Gauge 0 models after the adoption of the post-Grouping liveries. After the 1923 Grouping the new liveries had been introduced so quickly that the four new companies had not finalised their designs, and some Gauge 0 trains preserved anomalies such as the ampersand that was originally incorporated in the lettering of the L&NER. So it was to be again with the introduction of the new BR badge – Hornby accurately reproduced the badge as used by BR, whose policy was to have the lion facing forwards on both sides of the locomotive. This meant a different badge for each side, with the lion facing to the left in one and to the right in the other. But the College of Arms (which has been approving heraldic coats of arms since the 13th century) had only approved the left-facing badge, and persuaded BR to use this on both sides of its locomotives from 1960 onwards. Hornby

followed suit the same year, with the result that Hornby locomotives with the assymetrical badges (with the lion facing forwards on both sides) are another of the curiosities sought by collectors.

The year 1957 saw the launch of the 'Bristol Castle' locomotive, described by Michael Foster as being 'by general agreement the finest mass-produced commercial 00 gauge model locomotive ever produced to this day'. The real thing was also highly praised, designed by Charles Collett and acknowledged by railway historians as 'one of the most successful locomotives ever built for any railway'[iv] and as 'the handsomest and most efficient express engine to run in Britain'.[v] Collett was chief mechanical engineer of the GWR from 1922–41, and many of his best locomotives were improvements or enlargements of those of his predecessor George Jackson Churchward. The 4-6-0 Castle class was no exception, being an enlargement of Churchward's earlier Star class.

The first of the class,

'Caerphilly Castle', appeared at the British Empire Exhibition at Wembley in 1924, and was represented in Gauge 0 by one of Hornby's No 3 locomotives. An amazing 171 Castles were eventually built by the GWR (or converted from the Star class) between 1923 and 1950.

The Hornby-Dublo model was praised in almost equal measure to the real thing, and made a significant contribution to the aspect of model railways that has proved to be a blessing and a curse to Hornby ever since: it blurred the distinction between toy trains and model railways. Prior to 1957 there had been a significant difference between the two: 'ready to run' railways were seen as toys for the entertainment of children, while scale model railways were built from scratch by enthusiasts. Michael Foster points out that modellers would already have been hard pressed to match the detail of the Dublo A4s and Princess Coronations, but Hornby's 'Bristol Castle' was acknowledged by commentators on both sides of the argument to have considerably narrowed the gap between toys and models. The magazine *Model Railway*

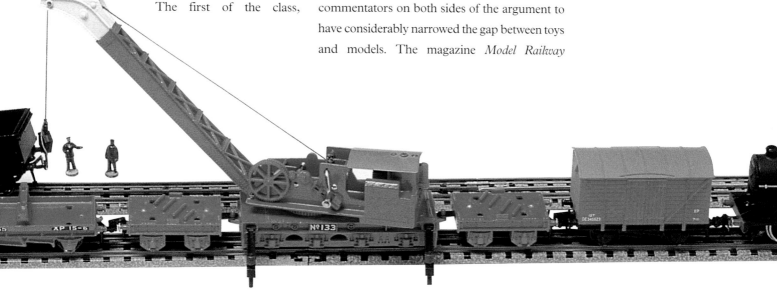

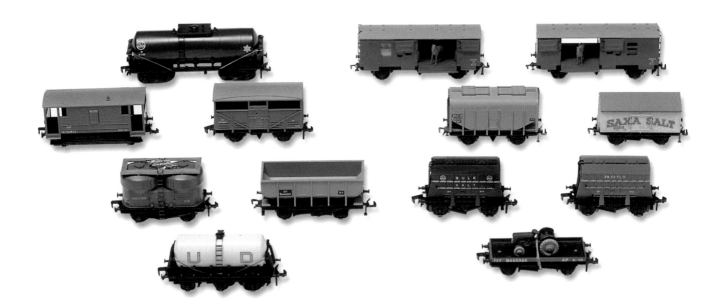

Above In 1958 Meccano launched a new range of super-detail moulded plastic goods wagons, beginning with the 20-ton bulk grain wagon pictured here alongside the Saxa Salt wagon. These new models were produced using high-quality tools manufactured by British Industrial Plastics, and quickly expanded into a comprehensive and popular range of goods wagons.

Constructor announced that 'not only have they produced a superlative locomotive at a most modest price but they have now bid fair to enter the scale model as well as the toy market', while the only criticism in the *Model Railway News* actually served to heighten the praise for the model overall: 'the flangeless wheels on the tender centre axle are horrible and are the only toylike touch to be found on the whole model'.

The introduction of Hornby's Castle class marked the beginning of Dublo's golden years in terms of quality, accuracy and performance (the 'Bristol Castle' was lauded for its technical and aesthetic prowess), but on the national network the full scale Castle class had been busy marking a series of endings. In 1936 No 4082 'Windsor Castle' hauled the funeral train of George V (who had driven the locomotive during his lifetime), and in 1952 'Windsor Castle' repeated the honour for George VI – except that it was not the same locomotive. The original 'Windsor Castle' was

being overhauled at the time of the King's death, and 'Bristol Castle', which had just been completed, assumed the name and number of the royal locomotive and took over the funeral duties. *Meccano Magazine* reported that 'Royal coats-of-arms on purple facings were carried on each side of the smoke-box during the journey to Windsor; the uppermost of the four headlamps was a special one surmounted by a Royal Crown'. The 'Bristol Castle' name and plates were fitted to the former 'Windsor Castle' after its overhaul, raising the interesting philosophical question of whether Hornby's 'Bristol Castle' actually represents the newer locomotive that was intended to be 'Bristol Castle' but became 'Windsor Castle', or the older locomotive that had been 'Windsor Castle' but became 'Bristol Castle'. Another closure marked by the real Castle class was that the last regular steam train to leave Paddington Station was hauled by No 7029 'Clun Castle' in November 1965.

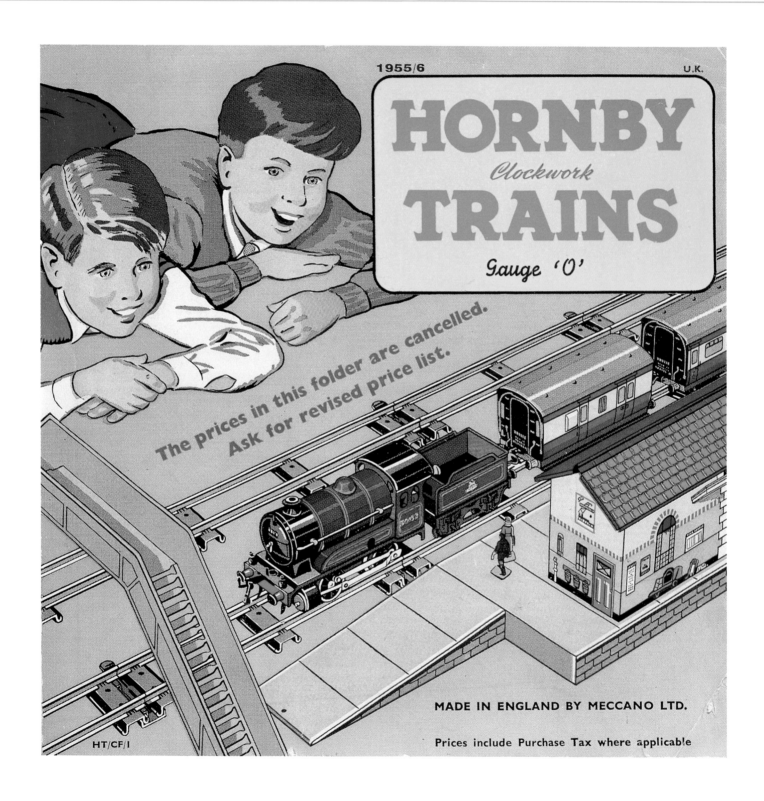

1955/6   U.K.

HORNBY
Clockwork
TRAINS
Gauge 'O'

The prices in this folder are cancelled.
Ask for revised price list.

MADE IN ENGLAND BY MECCANO LTD.

Prices include Purchase Tax where applicable

HT/CF/I

Above A selection of super-detail coaches, which were introduced from 1960 onwards. Each type of coach was released as its tinplate predecessor was phased out, with the super-detail restaurant cars and suburban coaches among the last to be introduced. This range of coaches had plastic ends and roofs with tinprinted sides and die-cast bogie sideframes.

As well as the 'Bristol Castle' locomotive, 1957 also saw the launch of Dublo scale Dinky Toys and the Travelling Post Office (TPO), one of Dublo's best-remembered items. This mail van was modelled closely on the real thing, and could pick up and drop off miniature mail bags on the move, as explained in great detail in *The Hornby Book of Trains*: 'The apparatus attached to a TPO of the present day for the exchange of mails includes a hinged net on the side of the vehicle for picking up the leather pouches in which the mail bags are packed, and several spring-governed arms called "traductors" from which pouches to be dropped are suspended. The ground apparatus consists of one or more standards from which the bags to be picked up by the train are hung, and a net to collect the bags from the traductors.' The Dublo TPO Mail Van Set was advertised thus: 'The Set comprises the Mail Van,

the lineside apparatus, two mail bags, and a push button switch to operate the mechanism . . . There is also a hut in which the postman on duty shelters while the exchange is taking place.'

Railway Modeller acknowledged the Travelling Post Office as a further narrowing of the gap between toys and models, reporting that 'although intended primarily for the popular proprietary system it is apparent to us that this model has possibilities in the field of pure scale models'. After such success with the standard of detailing in the 'Bristol Castle' and the TPO, Hornby again came up trumps the following year with a 20-ton bulk grain wagon. This may not sound like a particularly ground-breaking item but it was Dublo's first ever item of rolling stock to be made in plastic. Many people at the time and since have decried the change to plastic, but it allowed for far greater detail in the modelling, and in fact the bulk grain wagon was the first of a series of wagons and coaches marketed as the Super-Detail Rolling Stock.

Comparing the tinplate wagons with the new plastic wagons shows quite clearly that plastic lent itself far better to the detailing required, with doorhandles, hatches, ladders and the gaps between planks of wagons now possible in three dimensions instead of simply being printed on. *Model Railway Constructor* called the bulk grain wagon 'as revolutionary and as excellent in its way as the Castle . . . we heartily recommend this wagon to *all* 4 mm modellers and look forward eagerly to the other new items promised'. These promised items came thick and fast, and included an 8-ton cattle wagon, a 12-ton ventilated van, refrigerator van, Western Region goods brake van and, later, a horse box and various tanks and cement wagons. *Meccano Magazine* urged its

readers to check the details of the steel goods wagon 'through a magnifying glass. You will then realise that there is the best of reasons for the claim that nothing as fine in their line has ever been made than the astonishing moulded vehicles of the Hornby SD6 series'. And for once the model railway press was even more enthusiastic than the in-house magazine: *Model Railway Constructor* commented that 'the detail is exquisite and the neatness of the lettering will be the despair of all modellers who have had to do their own by hand', while *Railway Modeller* was lost for words, saying that 'we feel there is little we can add to previous remarks about this series of vehicles – we have virtually exhausted our stock of superlatives'.

These positive responses were vindication, if any were needed, for the use of moulded plastic (which was already being employed

Below Hornby's first diesel outline model, as well as the company's first plastic-bodied locomotive: the English Electric Type 1 Bo-Bo Diesel-Electric (top). For those who were unsure, Railway Modeller pointed out that the cab was, officially, at the back! Below is the similarly amorphous Class 08 0-6-0 Diesel Shunter, introduced two years later in 1960.

very successfully by a number of Hornby's competitors). The year 1958 also saw the announcement of the very first Dublo locomotive to be made from plastic rather than being die-cast. The English Electric Type 1 Bo-Bo Diesel-Electric Locomotive, as well as being the first plastic-bodied locomotive, was also significant in being the first diesel to be modelled by Hornby. Producing a diesel locomotive presented more of a sales risk to Hornby than might be supposed from a modern standpoint, when diesel and electric trains are commonplace: the move from steam to diesel on

the national railways was unpopular and it was thought that there might be no market for diesel trains among modellers. However, Meccano typically took the decision to follow real railway practice, and launched its diesel with the usual Meccano bravado: 'You've waited for it and it's worth it . . . Derived from the 1,000 hp British Railway type, that went into service last year, it is a finely detailed model with moulded body and die-cast bogies, superbly finished in British Railways colours. An exciting modern locomotive – a must for every up-to-date model railway.'

Diesel brought with it several changes, one of which was a new form of wheel notation in which each motorised axle was given a letter (A for one axle, B for two, etc.), and each carrying axle was given a number. This system (still in use) further differs from the Whyte notation used for steam locomotives in that where there are no carrying axles no zero is used, and where the motorised axles are driven separately an 'o' is added to the letter. Thus the new English Electric Type 1 modelled by Hornby was described as Bo-Bo, having no leading axles, two bogies, each with two separately driven axles, and no trailing axles.

Once again the use of plastic had its detractors, but the wealth of detail that plastic made possible overcame most of the doubts, and Hornby's first version of the Bo-Bo Diesel-Electric proved to be a very successful model despite the somewhat characterless shape of the original. *Model Railway Constructor* commented that 'the wealth and quality of detail included in the moulded body gives this model much more interest and character than would have been thought possible from the shapeless outline and boxlike appearance which diesel locomotives

1953/4

in general seem to possess', while the *Railway Modeller* felt constrained to point out that 'the cab is, officially, at the back of the locomotive'! Hornby's first model was D8000, the first of the BR series of which 97 were eventually built.

In the same year as the Bo-Bo Diesel-Electric, Hornby also introduced the celebrated 2-8-0 8F freight locomotive, much to the excitement of *Railway Modeller*, which announced: 'Two new Hornby-Dublo locos. So soon after the

would prove immensely popular: a Meccano dealers' leaflet for August 1958 reported that supplies could not keep up with demand and that there would be 'some unavoidable delay in dealing with current orders'.

While Hornby was keeping pace with the modernisation of the real railways by introducing the Bo-Bo diesel-electric locomotive in 1958, the company was also embarking on a modernisation plan of its own. In January 1959 an

Below Two- and three-rail versions of the 8F. Hornby often had whimsical reasons for choosing the running numbers of its models, some representing the company telephone number or jumbled up versions of the date of release. The first 8F to be represented was No 48158, a real BR running number – coincidentally or not, the model was released in 1958.

introduction of the "Castle" come two more first-class locomotives!' The 8F, originally designed by William Stanier for the LMS and introduced in 1935, was a popular choice of locomotive to model because a massive 849 had been built and put into use on all regions of British Railways after nationalisation. *Model Railway Constructor* said of the 8F that 'This really is a beautiful model and we have purposely devoted two photographs to it', while *Model Railway News* said that 'It is a very pleasing model, full of character and should prove immensely popular; it has already won our approval.' *MRN* was right in thinking that it

advertisement in *Meccano Magazine* urged readers to: 'Make 1959 "Modernisation Year" on your Railway'. The advertisement continued by saying that 'you can start your own modernisation plans by installing up-to-the-minute Colour Light Signalling on your Hornby-Dublo railway', but colour light signals were among the lesser changes in store for 1959, because this was the year in which two-rail track and locomotives were introduced.

Prior to 1959, Dublo had followed the Gauge 0 system of three-rail track with a centre-rail pick-up, and the introduction of a two-rail system was

Opposite page top One of the most contentious moves made by Meccano was the introduction of two-rail track in 1959. This innovation was intended to save the Hornby-Dublo system but, according to one school of thought, was the cause of its downfall.

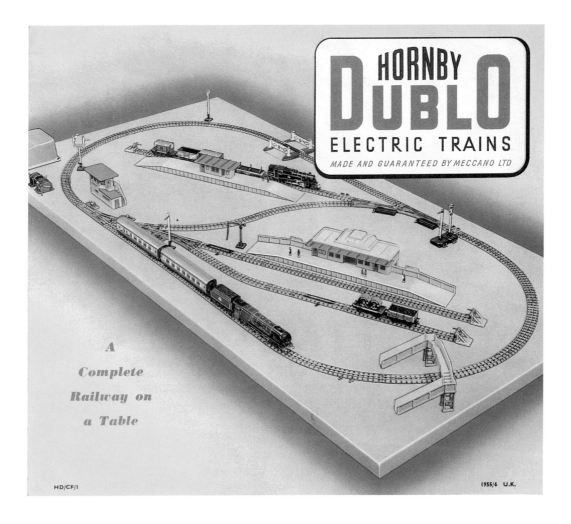

perhaps the most important single development that Hornby was to introduce to Dublo – even more so than the introduction of moulded plastic locomotives and rolling stock. Meccano began to run into financial problems shortly after the introduction of the two-rail system, and there are three schools of thought as to why. Purists claim that two-rail was the downfall of Dublo because it did not work as well as three-rail; modernisers claim that it was a necessary step forward but that it came too late; and pragmatists hold that the main problem was trying to run the two systems

side by side. (Hornby had little choice but to continue manufacturing three-rail track and locomotives in order not to alienate its existing customers, while pressing ahead with an expensive two-rail system at the same time.)

The person perhaps best qualified to comment is Ronald Wyborn, ex-chief electrical engineer for the company, who regrets that two-rail had not been used from the inception of Dublo in 1938 rather than taking the easier option of copying the Märklin system. That said, many of Hornby's competitors were still using three-rail

systems in 1959 – the main reason for change was growing competition from Tri-ang, who (as Rovex) had launched a more realistic-looking two-rail system in 1950 with enormous and immediate success.

Realism had always been an important factor in model railways, and *Railway Modeller* warmly approved of Hornby's adoption of the two-rail system, saying that it was 'well worth the wait, for here we have a "toy" system which is virtually in every respect a scale model railway'. Theatre director Max Stafford-Clark remembers changing to the two-rail system: 'I was always a fan of Hornby-Dublo but they did have three rails, which was rather a drawback. There was a

centre rail to pick up the current, and that seemed very unrealistic, and so I did want to swap it to two-rail, which I did at some point.' He describes his ongoing interest in model railways as:

...a sporadic obsession. When the fever grips me I'll be in the model shop every Saturday afternoon, and I'll usually buy something ... It's a private world, and I think that people need something that's akin to meditation. Fishing is the biggest hobby in the country. I see no attraction in fishing but I can understand that sitting there on a riverbank is the nearest you ever get to facing yourself, that kind of contemplation of an inner world. Trains are a bit like that, too. It wasn't a world I ever wanted to share with anyone else, it was a private world I could retire to. It's a private world you can make perfect, I suppose a bit like my attempts in the theatre.

The Hornby-Dublo two-rail system was introduced in March 1959, and just six months later Meccano claimed that it was 'already accepted as the finest model railway track ever produced' – but then, they would. A more

Left The Terminus and Through Station Composite Kit, introduced in 1961 and set up here as a terminal station, was one of the very few Hornby-Dublo items to be carried over into the Tri-ang Hornby range after the take-over by Lines Bros in 1964.

Below The popular R1 Tank Locomotive, which Railway Modeller predicted would 'sell like hot cakes' – the magazine was right about the black model but the green version, which had been introduced to add colour to a range dominated by BR's black livery, did not sell well.

ay operation is the expansion of the system
wner is well catered for. Starting with one
ils) an excellent variety of wagons, coaches,
remote-controlled signals and other details

ow, in which a wide selection of accessories

E TAX

Y-DUBLO ACCESSORIES

	£ s. d.
Junction, Electrically	
Home" or "Distant"	15 6
dge .	17 11
	2 5 0
n	15 6
sing	9 6
auge	2 9
ngle Arm, "Home" or	
orm	1 5 0
ne	1 9
orm Extension	7 6
et of 6 (Dinky Toys No.	
	3 0
et of 6 (Dinky Toys No.	
	3 0
tation	2 10 0
Single Arm, Electrically	
Home" or "Distant"	9 11
	2 4
	10 9
tation Platform Extension	11 6
ble Arm	3 6
nction "Home" or "Dis-	
	3 11
Double Arm, Electrically	
	14 6

The prefix numbers
printed in red relate
to the respective
components featur-
ed in the railway
layout below.

Gauge 00— $\frac{5}{8}$in. (16.5 mm.)

Above How many fingers? Advertising
Manager Harold Owens must have had a
bump on the head before preparing the
1957 catalogue.

objective view, and just as positive, is provided by a retrospective review of track by the *Model Railway Constructor* published in 1965, which described two-rail Dublo track as 'the most realistic of the "big three" proprietary tracks' and, furthermore, 'it was sturdy and reliable in operation'. (Although this is a matter of opinion – today the track is notorious among collectors for being somewhat flimsy.)

And, of course, new track meant new locomotives – the entire Dublo stable was reworked for two-rail operation, and two new 0-6-0 R1 Tank Locomotives were launched to start the new system, one in green livery and another one in black. The previous new locomotive had been the up-to-the-minute Bo-Bo Diesel-Electric, but the R1 Tanks recalled the fast disappearing days of steam, having been first introduced to the South Eastern Railway as the R 0-6-0 in 1888 (later rebuilds were designated R1). The South Eastern Railway eventually became part of the Southern Region of British Railways at nationalisation, and the R1 class tanks remained in service until April 1960, the year after the Dublo versions appeared. The last of the R1 Tanks in operation were used to haul boat trains up and down the 1-in-30 incline at Folkestone harbour, where the South Eastern Railway had set up a cross-channel service back in 1845. (This service was said to have shortened the life of Charles Dickens, after he was involved in an accident at Staplehurst in 1865 caused by a misunderstanding over timings of the tide.)

Hornby's models, numbered to match two of the last survivors, were No 31340 (in green) and No 31337 (in black), both with the British Rail 'lion-and-crown' badge (with the lion facing forwards on both sides). But while Hornby's new tank locomotives may have recalled days gone by

Left Early examples of Dublo Dinky Toys, '00' scale vehicles introduced in 1957 as trackside accessories for Dublo railway layouts.

Below West Country class locomotives 'Barnstaple' (two-rail) and 'Dorchester' (three-rail), which were criticised by the model railway press and failed to catch the imagination of the public.

on the real railways, they were right up to date in terms of Dublo, sharing one thing in common with the Bo-Bo – they were made of moulded plastic. The associated Goods Set comprised existing super-detail wagons, and for the Passenger Set Hornby introduced new tinplate suburban coaches in Southern Region green, replaced by super-detail SR coaches at the end of the following year.

The next two-rail locomotive was an updated version of the Princess Coronation (Duchess) class, previously represented in three-rail by the 'Duchess of Atholl' in LMS livery and the 'Duchess of Montrose' in BR livery. The new addition was locomotive No 46245 'City of London' in the new BR standard red, which in fact matched the original LMS red. The full-scale 'City of London' had been repainted in its new colour at the end of 1957, but for the Dublo model this did not simply mean a new paint finish on the existing 'Duchess of Montrose' mould, or a reversion to the 'Duchess of Atholl': the entire body was recast for the 'City of London', and fitted with the new two-rail motor. The new body-casing and BR red livery were made available in a

three-rail version during 1961, when No 46274 'City of Liverpool' replaced the 'Duchess of Montrose' in the catalogue.

Soon afterwards the rest of the three-rail locomotive types became available in two-rail versions: the A4 Pacific, previously represented by 'Sir Nigel Gresley' (LNER), 'Silver King' (BR) and 'Mallard' (BR), was represented in two-rail by No 60030 'Golden Fleece'; the Castle class, previously represented by the renowned 'Bristol Castle', became available as No 7032 'Denbigh Castle'; and the unnamed locomotives were all issued in two-rail carrying new running numbers. The only failure among all of these innovations was the two-rail version of the Bo-Bo Diesel-Electric, D8017, that appeared in 1960: a combination of factors meant that this model did not run smoothly, largely due to poor current collection, with the result that it was withdrawn from the catalogues during 1962 and never reintroduced.

In the midst of this busy period for locomotives, Hornby also introduced various new accessories, including several new Dublo Dinky Toys, a new power unit and various trackside

buildings and
effects. The company was also
developing a new motor, the Ring Field Motor,
which was first introduced during 1960 in a new
Dublo Castle class locomotive, No 4075 'Cardiff
Castle'. In order to publicise the hardiness of the
new motor Meccano organised an 'endurance
test' at the company's London office, the
challenge being for the Dublo version of the
'Cardiff Castle' to travel 145 miles, the same as
the distance travelled by the Red Dragon Express
from London to Cardiff. The start of the
challenge was witnessed by John Gale, one of
BR's Red Dragon drivers, and by the time he
returned four days later to watch the finish of this
remarkable feat of endurance the Dublo model
had made 46,000 circuits of the track, exceeding
expectations by travelling 153 actual miles,
11,663 scale miles – an achievement which was
later recorded in the *Guinness Book of Records*.
Meccano Magazine's write-up of the event
pointed out that 'in the whole of this four-day
marathon of non-stop running, the Ring Field
Motor, which is to be fitted to several Hornby-
Dublo locomotives this season, did not falter nor
did it require the slightest attention'.

The other
locomotives to appear, as
promised, with the new Ring Field Motor
included a new 8F freight locomotive, No 48073,
and two entirely new models, the English Electric
Co-Co Diesel-Electric (aka the 'Deltic') and the
0-6-0 Diesel Shunter. The Deltic was named after
its engine, which had originally been developed
by D Napier & Son in order to be used in naval
patrol boats. Twenty-two Deltics were built for
British Rail following the success of a one-off
prototype that had been built by English Electric
as a private venture, and at the time they were
built they were the world's most powerful
locomotives. Never shy of a publicity stunt,
Meccano showed that the Dublo Deltic with its
Ring Field Motor was also a world-beater, by
demonstrating the Hornby model hauling a 2.5-
stone child along a track on a specially
constructed trolley weighing another half stone!

Hornby actually managed to produce the
Dublo model of the Deltic before all the details
of the real thing had been finalised, leading to one

Above Two- and three-rail versions of the
'Deltic', a locomotive which cleverly
circumvented the most serious drawback
of earlier diesels – that of knowing which
end was which. The 'Deltic' was more
reminiscent of Hugh Lofting's Pushmi-
Pullyu than the racehorses after which
some of the class were named.

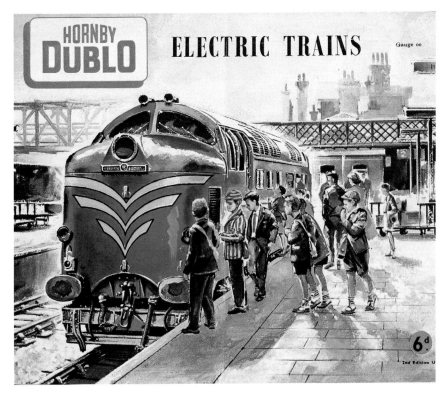

HORNBY DUBLO ELECTRIC TRAINS Gauge oo 6d 2nd Edition U

or two discrepancies in the Dublo version, not least of which was the incomplete livery. Correctly liveried versions were launched during 1962, the two-rail version being No D9012 'Crepello' and the three-rail No D9001 'St Paddy', both named after racehorses – Crepello had won the 2,000 Guineas and the 1957 Derby, while St Paddy had won the 1960 Derby, St Leger and 2,000 Guineas.

While the new Deltic reverted to former Meccano practice of a die-cast body, the 0-6-0 Diesel Shunter continued the newer practice of high-impact moulded plastic, which allowed a huge amount of detail to be included on the model. But despite the wealth of detail, the Dublo shunters (D3763 for three-rail and D3302 for two-rail, both in BR green livery) were one of Meccano's less successful models. The motors had a tendency to overheat, the two-rail version did not run smoothly, and *Model Railway Constructor* complained that neither version could haul more than six super-detail coaches. The same *MRC* article remarked that 'Despite the present popularity, amounting to almost universal use, of two-rail electrification, Meccano Ltd have not forgotten their earlier followers who are still using three-rail equipment and have introduced three-rail versions of both the "Deltic" Co-Co main line diesel locomotive and the the 0-6-0 shunting locomotive.' Good for customer relations but bad for economics, and many model railway historians maintain that it was Meccano's attempts to run the two systems in parallel that led to the eventual downfall of the company a short time later.

New products in 1961 included new super-detail Pullman cars, sleeping cars, passenger

coaches and goods wagons, and two new locomotives, both die-cast and both available in two- and three-rail versions. One of these was the 4-6-2 West Country class steam locomotive, once more recalling the days of steam after the previous year's forays into the world of diesel. The original West Country class was designed by Oliver Bulleid for the Southern Railway and introduced in 1945 – as with Gauge 0, Southern Railway fans had had to wait longer than most for their main line locomotive. Bulleid, who had been apprenticed to Henry Ivatt and been assistant to Nigel Gresley, produced 140 Pacifics for the SR, 30 of the famous Merchant Navy class and 110 of the slightly smaller West Country (or Battle of Britain) class, two feet shorter than the Merchant Navies and light enough to be used throughout the area covered by the Southern Railway (later BR's Southern Region). The Merchant Navy class was modified from 1956 with such success that 60 of the West Country class were also rebuilt, resulting in the profile of the Hornby-Dublo models. The three-rail version was No 34005 'Barnstaple' and the two-rail No 34042 'Dorchester', both of which were criticised in the model railway press for lack of attention to details such as the size of the chimney and driving wheels and the type of tender. 'Barnstaple' did not prove

overly popular with the public either, selling little more than a tenth of the number produced.

The other new locomotive to appear in 1961, the Co-Bo Diesel-Electric, fared even worse, selling only 4 per cent of stocks – a sure sign of a decline in sales and one that should have been increasingly difficult to ignore, although the Meccano directors managed to do so until it was far too late. The *Model Railway Constructor* review of this unpopular model ended with what could have been seen as either a backhanded compliment or a sugar-coated criticism of Hornby trains, saying that British manufacturers would only meet the standards of their European competitors when they combined the excellence of Meccano's Ring Field Motor with the high detail of moulded plastic body casings: again, significant in light of the fact that Hornby's two latest offerings had reverted to die-cast bodies despite the success of earlier plastic locomotives.

It is interesting that *Model Railway Constructor* should have made the comparison with European manufacturers in the year that Meccano began to import Hornby H0 gauge locomotives and coaches manufactured in its French factory. The imports were made to test the British market response to H0, or Acho as it was branded by Hornby (pronounced aitch-o, not ack-o: similarly

Below The Southern Region electric suburban train, otherwise known as an Electric Multiple Unit, or EMU. The Hornby-Dublo EMU was originally intended as a three-car unit but this proved too expensive and it eventually reached the shops as a two-car set which could be extended to the standard three-car formation by the addition of the Dublo super-detail second class suburban coach, as seen here.

Opposite page Schoolchildren and adults alike crowd around the 'Deltic'.

Gauge OO

H C

THE PERFECT

The remarkable success of the Hornby-Dublo Railway introduced last year has proved our claim that this is the finest system in the world for the development of a complete miniature railway where space is limited. The trains are actually one seventy-sixth of the size of real trains, and are marvellous scale models of their prototypes.

Hornby-Dublo electric locomotives are fitted for remote control; starting, stopping, reversing and speed regulation are all carried out from the lineside by the movement of a single lever. All Hornby-Dublo coaches, vans and wagons have automatic couplings.

The great new feature of the Hornby-Dublo System this year is the introduction of Isolating Rails for dividing a layout into separate sections that can be made

This attra
the Hornby-D
line serving t
yet the whole
8 ft. x 4 ft.

By means
be operated i
shunt wagons
while the stre
or the goods
Signals are e

BLE RAILWAY

"alive" or "dead" as desired. By means of these Rails, and special Switches (D2), endless fun can be had by controlling two or more trains independently at the same time. All kinds of interesting shunting operations can be carried out, every movement being made as on real railways.

Other new features include Electrically-Operated Points, and large radius Curved Rails, which, used in conjunction with the standard Dublo Rails, form a perfect double track.

Hornby-Dublo electric trains operate on Direct Current at 12 volts. This current may be obtained in three different ways—first, from Alternating Current mains supply through a Dublo Transformer and a Dublo Controller No. 1; second, from Direct Current mains supply through a D.C. Converter and a Dublo Controller No. 1; third, from Accumulators giving 12 volts, with a Dublo Controller No. 1A.

layout shows the splendid possibilities of System. There is a double track main tions, and an interesting goods yard, and commodated on a board measuring only

lating Rails and Switches the trains can ndently of one another. An engine can e goods yard in the centre of the layout ed express dashes round the inner road, runs round the outer track. Points and ally operated from special Switches.

Below The Co-Bo Diesel-Electric, which was the least successful locomotive in the entire Hornby-Dublo range in terms of sales. Based on an unprepossessing box-like original, the model reverted to a die-cast body and was criticised for a lack of fine detail, leading to calls in the model railway press for British manufacturers to adopt moulded plastic bodies as standard practice.

to Dublo, it was the phonetic form of H0). Hornby-Acho was first shown at the Nuremburg Toy Fair in 1960 where it was much praised for its quietness and smooth-running. It was introduced in France as the successor to Gauge 0, where an internal memo announced that 'we certainly hope, indeed, to be able to manufacture our two trains alongside each other for many years, for the 0 will be aimed in particular at our younger customers (5 to 10 year olds) while the H0 will suit the older ones better'.[vi] Acho received good reviews on its introduction to Britain, and Binns Road even considered improving its own rolling stock to meet the standards of the French Acho, although this was never implemented. Similarly to Dublo in Britain, Acho flourished for a while due to the quality of manufacture but eventually sank due to uncompetitive costs (and, therefore, prices). Production continued until 1973.

Meanwhile, back in Britain, 1962 saw the introduction of the Southern Region Suburban Electric Trains, although by the end of the year the introduction of new models looked absurd in the

light of the fact that Meccano share prices had dropped by a third and the company was unable to pay an interim dividend – this compared with profits of more than a quarter of a million pounds the previous year and dividends of 9 per cent. The Suburban Electric Train was well received, although the *Model Railway Constructor* review again questioned Meccano's resistance to change: 'Knowing the reluctance of Hornby to change from metal to plastic sides, we were not surprised to find the printed tin sides had been perpetuated; we are pleased to see, however, that the outer ends of the driving vehicles are fitted with a most realistic moulded plastic front end'.

These suburban electric trains, known as multiple units, were introduced to the railways under BR's modernisation programmes. Because they were self-powered their introduction led to a large reduction in the number of trains hauled by locomotives, which in turn provided huge advantages in the logistics of passenger transport, radically reducing the need for shunting movements. Furthermore, as pointed out in the *Tri-ang Hornby Book of Trains*, 'no problem arises when extra stock is required at periods of peak traffic, for each additional set brings with it its own tractive power, and the total power available is always commensurate with the number of coaches on the train'.

The late 20th century saw the introduction of the phrase 'panic buying' into the language, but for Meccano 1963 was a year of panic selling. Or, at least, panic marketing – selling was the big problem. The company offered huge prizes, including cars and foreign holidays, to winners of the dealer's Hornby-Dublo Window Display

Competition, and prizes of trains or cash to new buyers who could give the judges the best three reasons for buying their set. The eventual winner, announced in the April 1964 *Meccano Magazine*, was 13-year-old Andrew Farthing, who listed his three reasons as being: '1. The best buys are Horn-buys. 2. I double my pleasure with Dublo treasures. 3. Their "realistic railway replicas" are the three R's for boys'. Ironically, by the time the winner's name was announced, the best buys were no longer Horn-buys because by then the company had been bought by Lines Bros, owners of Meccano's main competitors Tri-ang.

A more sensible approach to the serious inroads being made by competitors such as Tri-ang and Playcraft, though introduced far too late, was the 0-4-0 Starter Set. It had been standard practice for Meccano to include cheaper sets in the Gauge 0 series in order to attract brand loyalty from model railway beginners, but they had neglected to do the same for Dublo. The result of this omission was that more and more younger children were starting out with Tri-ang or Playcraft and then sticking with them. The Dublo 0-4-0 Starter Set was introduced as the solution to this problem, and comprised a plastic-bodied generic 0-4-0 tank locomotive (in black with BR badges), two goods wagons, a brake van and a circle of track. The revolutionary feature was that the set also included a power unit and controller, providing everything in one box that a beginner would need to set up a simple system –

Right 'Bristol Castle' appeared on the cover of the 1957 Hornby-Dublo Catalogue.

the system was marketed under the heading 'Ready to Run'. The Starter Sets sold well but it was too late to reverse the tide of commercial disaster that was already upon Meccano. Later variations of the starter locomotives included a generic yellow 0-4-0 diesel shunter adapted from the Dublo BR standard 0-6-0 shunter (which had sold poorly), and a surprising late addition in March 1964: the last steam locomotive to be produced by Meccano was a blue version of the 0-4-0 tank locomotive badged with a map of Australia and the word 'Commonwealth' on the tank's sides.

The last new Dublo locomotive of all, available in October 1964, was the E3000 Pantograph Electric Locomotive. A pantograph is the retractable assembly on the roof of the locomotive used to collect current from the overhead wires. The Dublo version, E3002, was designed to operate either from the two-rail track or from a system of overhead wires known as a catenary, although Dublo had no catenary system available. Ironically Tri-ang did have a catenary system, and by the time this model became available Tri-ang and Hornby were stablemates rather than competitors, so the publicity

photographs for the Hornby locomotive showed it running under the Tri-ang catenary. The Hornby-Dublo model proved so successful that it actually delayed the release of the proposed Tri-ang model (numbered E3001), which was modified to use parts of the Dublo model.

With hindsight it is possible to recognise that Gauge 0 reached its zenith in 1937 with the 'Princess Elizabeth', although at the time it was hoped that the excellence of the model was a sign of more to come. In the same way, hindsight reveals that Dublo's greatest achievements came between 1957 and 1960 with the 'Bristol Castle', the introduction of super-detailed rolling stock, and the development of the universally acclaimed Ring Field Motor. The popular introduction of two-rail track and Dublo Starter Sets, and the more controversial introduction of plastic-bodied locomotives, came too late to save Meccano from a downward spiral of financial decline. On 14 February 1964 Lines Bros, the owners of Meccano's greatest competitor Tri-ang Railways, bought Meccano for £781,000 and, almost inevitably, Hornby-Dublo ended as Gauge 0 had done – not with a bang but a whimper.

Below The end of an era – the last Hornby-Dublo locomotive was the E3000 Pantograph Electric Locomotive, otherwise known as the Class AL1 or Class 81, seen here alongside an unfinished pre-production sample rescued from the scrap bin by a Meccano employee.

i Toy Trains
ii As quoted in Hornby-Dublo Trains
iii Hornby-Dublo Trains
iv Observer's Book of Railway Locomotives
v British Railways' Steam Locomotives
vi Internal Memo by Andre Rio, quoted in Michael Foster's Hornby-Dublo Trains

From
'Tri-ang
Hornby'
to
'Hornby
Railways'

It was on St Valentine's Day 1964 that Lines Bros Ltd, the owners of Hornby-Dublo's greatest competitor Tri-ang Railways, bought Meccano Ltd – but the match was not made in heaven, and there was certainly no love lost between fans of Hornby-Dublo and its 'new overlord', as Tri-ang was described by one irate correspondent to the *Model Railway Constructor*. In fact the correspondent was aiming his vitriol at the wrong target: Tri-ang never bought Hornby. The following points should clarify the matter, or at least bring the complications into the open: 'Tri-ang', like 'Hornby', was a brand name; Tri-ang Railways were manufactured by Rovex Scale Models Ltd (as it was known in 1964), which was owned by Lines Bros Ltd; Lines Bros Ltd bought Meccano Ltd, which manufactured Hornby trains, and this meant that Tri-ang and Hornby were both now brands manufactured by member companies of the Lines Bros empire – Tri-ang did not own Hornby.

For fans of Hornby-Dublo, though, it seemed as if their system had been hijacked by its greatest rival. (A rival whose name was a pun on that of the 'new overlords'. The Tri-ang trade-name was coined by the three Lines brothers who had originally formed Lines Bros – three lines, as everyone knows, form a Tri-angle.) 1964 was a year of confusion and 'wait-and-see'. Rumours were rife as to what Lines Bros would do with Hornby, and in the meantime both Hornby-Dublo and Tri-ang Railways released new products, as detailed in their catalogues which had been prepared the previous year. For Hornby, the new products included the concept of Track Packs, a woefully belated attempt to sell 'Simplec', a simplified version of the Dublo two-rail track which in its original form had proved too complicated for general use.

However, the two systems were not to continue in parallel for much longer. Lines Bros now owned two competing brands, and circumstances were such that they could not continue to exist side by side in the marketplace. Richard Lines is the son of one of the original Lines brothers and was responsible for Rovex Scale Models Ltd at the time. Nearly 40 years later he remembers the situation: 'We had two lots of trains of the same scale and the same voltage but they were not actually completely integratable because the track fixings were different and the couplings were different and so on.' But for those who claim that Lines Bros shut down the Hornby-Dublo production line in order to dispose of the competition, Richard Lines's answer is quite clear:

When I first went up to Binns Road and looked round I was not unduly surprised to find that they had stopped making trains altogether. Nothing was happening in the train room. There were considerable stocks of finished goods but they'd actually stopped production altogether. If they'd been busy making trains we would have had to decide whether to change them or what on earth to do . . . The problem with a system like a model railway is that you can't readily change anything because it all has to be compatible.

Public reaction (at least from the vociferous fans of Hornby-Dublo) seemed to demand that Rovex cease manufacture of Tri-ang Railways in order to take over production of Dublo, a highly unlikely scenario given that there were huge stocks of unsold Dublo items sitting at the Binns Road factory, and that the commercial failure of Dublo (despite its high quality) was one of the

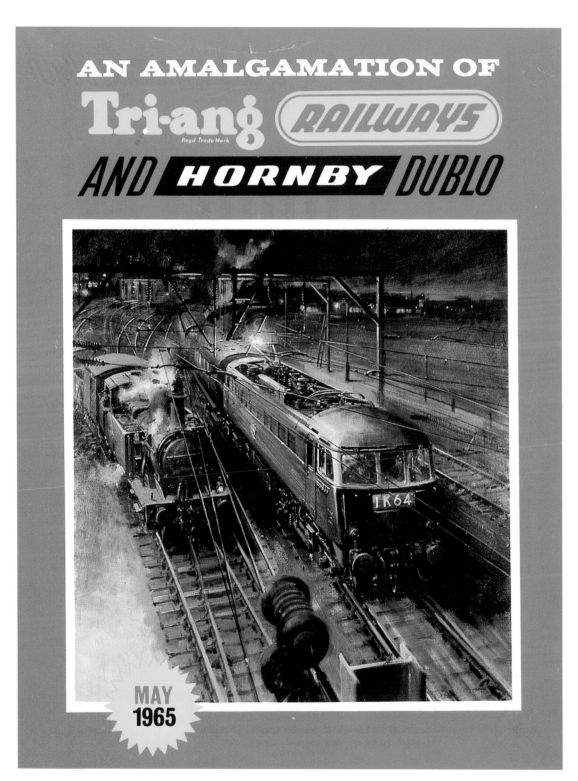

AN AMALGAMATION OF Tri-ang RAILWAYS AND HORNBY DUBLO

Regd Trade Mark

MAY 1965

Left What's in a name? The Tri-ang Railways and Hornby Dublo 'amalgamation' leaflet heralding the attachment of the Hornby name to the Tri-ang system.

Below The Terminus and Through Station Composite Kit was one of only two models from the Hornby-Dublo system to be absorbed into the Tri-ang Hornby range and be manufactured at Margate.

contributing factors to the failure of Meccano. In February 1965, a full year after the take-over, *Railway Modeller* put the thoughts of many model railway fans into print: 'The big question is, of course, what will happen to Hornby Dublo.' Three months later came the answer: a Lines Bros leaflet entitled 'An Amalgamation of Tri-ang Railways and Hornby-Dublo'.

The amalgamation leaflet tried to give the impression that the Lines Bros take-over would result in just that – an amalgamation of the two systems. Interviewed in *Model Railway Constructor* in 1966, Richard Lines said that 'we came to the conclusion that it was desirable to amalgamate the systems and convert certain Hornby-Dublo items so that they could be fully integrated with Tri-ang models'. The introduction to the amalgamation leaflet seemed to tell the same story of proposed integration: 'The two railways will, therefore, be progressively brought together under the name Tri-ang Hornby.' However, the following paragraph of the

introduction contradicted the idea of a 'coming together': 'Existing owners of Hornby-Dublo will continue to be able to purchase Hornby-Dublo components while stocks last . . .' In other words, production of Hornby-Dublo would not be restarted. This was not to be an amalgamation, in fact, but a phasing out of the unprofitable Dublo range.

The amalgamation leaflet included seven former Hornby-Dublo locomotives as part of the new Tri-ang Hornby range, as well as a Terminus and Through Station Composite Kit, and several other accessories. The locomotives were the West Country class 'Barnstaple', the Co-Bo Diesel-Electric, the Co-Co Deltic (which was not illustrated), the N2 Tank, the R1 Tank, the 0-6-0 Diesel Shunter and the E3000 Electric Pantograph Locomotive. The inclusion of the 'Barnstaple' and the Co-Bo diesel-electric locomotive was something of a surprise as both had been so unpopular, but it was seen as a good way of trying to shift some of the unsold stock. Five of these locomotives (the E3000 and the Co-Co Deltic being the exceptions) were offered 'complete with a Tri-ang Hornby Converter Wagon at no extra cost so that it can be used with Tri-ang Railways or Hornby-Dublo rolling stock'.

The Converter Wagon was based on the existing Tri-ang Railways Seven-Plank Open Wagon, modified to have a Hornby-Dublo coupling at one end while retaining the existing Tri-ang tension-lock coupling at the other. The wagon was a very simple and successful means of allowing Dublo locomotives to haul Tri-ang goods wagons and vice-versa, as explained in the amalgamation leaflet: 'Tri-ang Railways Tension-Lock Couplings operate vertically while

Hornby-Dublo couplings operate horizontally . . . the Converter Wagon is now introduced to allow users of either system to operate mixed Freight Trains.' The leaflet also promised that 'A passenger converter vehicle will be introduced when Hornby-Dublo Passenger coaches cease to be available' – in the event this took the form of a horse box, being a wagon that could logically be pulled as part of a passenger train while cleverly avoiding the need for converter versions of each type of coach. Another important item for those who were integrating their systems was the Converter Track, which allowed Tri-ang's Super 4 track to be connected to Hornby-Dublo two-rail track. Fortunately, all of the Hornby locomotives and rolling stock, and most of the Tri-ang range, would operate on either type of track.

The provision of converter wagons turned out not to be an interim measure pending the modification of the existing Hornby-Dublo locomotives and rolling stock; it was actually an interim measure pending their disappearance from the catalogue. The five locomotives available with the Converter Wagon remained in the catalogue until stocks ran out (within a year in the case of the N2 Tank), and the only Hornby-Dublo items that were actually incorporated into the

Tri-ang Hornby range were the Terminus and Through Station Kit and the E3000 Locomotive. Tri-ang's planned pantograph locomotive was abandoned in favour of the superb Hornby-Dublo model, which carried the running number E3002 and was modified to become the Tri-ang Hornby Class 81 Pantograph Locomotive with the running number E3001. The reason for the change of classification was that the E3000 (itself a misnomer, because the first of the class was numbered E3001) was more correctly known as the AL1, a term later updated to Class 81.

The Tri-ang Hornby version retained the body moulding of the Hornby-Dublo model but used the Tri-ang bogie power unit fitted knurled wheels, which made for noisy running, one of the factors picked up by the reviewer for *Railway Modeller*, who said that: 'The new Tri-ang Hornby 00 gauge AL1 25kV "Blue Electric" loco No "E3001" is a very satisfactory model of the earliest of the locomotives for the LMR electrification. The proportions are correct and there are some very pleasing small touches – for example the characteristic large buffers of the prototype are fitted. The performance and hauling power are good, but the loco, being fitted with knurled wheels, is rather noisy.' Another

Above The railroad to Damascus? Converter track with Hornby two-rail connectors at one end and Tri-ang Super 4 connectors at the other, allowing the two track systems to be joined together. Similarly, the Converter Wagons had Hornby-Dublo couplings at one end and Tri-ang couplings at the other, enabling locomotives of either make to haul the rolling stock of the other.

alteration from the Hornby-Dublo version was that the plug used to change the current collection from overhead catenary to track was replaced with a much smaller and neater switch, although this was still too obtrusive for the *Railway Modeller*. However, obtrusive switch or not, the fact that the model could collect current either from the track or from an overhead catenary meant that two locomotives could be operated on a single track, which added to the popularity of the model. Later versions of the E3001 had only one pantograph, reflecting BR's decision to remove one from each locomotive – the network Class 81s usually ran with one pantograph extended and one collapsed, but BR soon discovered that both required equal maintenance and therefore removed one in order to reduce maintenance costs.

Given that only two Hornby-Dublo items became part of the new range, 'Tri-ang Hornby' was an amalgamation in name only. Nonetheless, it was a wise move on the part of Lines Bros to bow to public pressure and adopt the Hornby name rather than alienating many of its new

customers. Lines Bros had bought Meccano not only to add to the company's range of products (with Dinky Toys and Meccano itself), but also for its name and reputation. Although Dublo had failed commercially, the Hornby brand was part of Meccano's reputation, and for Rovex to associate a name that had been a market leader for 45 years with the relatively young Tri-ang brand added a great deal of kudos to the range. But while the Hornby name provided the gravitas, Rovex provided the modern approach to manufacture and marketing, which meant that the Tri-ang Hornby range (with the exception of the E3000/Class 81 Electric) followed the development path of the earlier Tri-ang Railways products rather than that of Hornby-Dublo. In order to understand the pedigree of the railway system that from now on would carry the Hornby name, it is necessary to back-track to 1946, when Alexander Venetzian founded Rovex Plastics Ltd.

Venetzian, who had previously been a racing driver for Mercedes-Benz, manufactured high-quality plastic toys exclusively for Marks & Spencer, and in 1950 his company produced the first Rovex train set, based on the former LMS 'Princess Elizabeth' in black BR livery. After some teething problems this train set proved so successful that it was recognised as having the potential to form the basis of a complete model railway system, but financial constraints prevented Rovex from developing it any further. In the meantime, Lines Bros Ltd, trading as Tri-ang, wanted to break into the post-World War II model railways market. Rovex needed capital to develop its model railway system, and Lines Bros had plenty of capital, so Lines Bros bought Rovex. A new system was developed remarkably quickly and was relaunched as Tri-ang Railways at the British Industries Fair in May 1952.

In order to produce a range of products quickly, Rovex bought the tools for a goods train set manufactured by Pyramid Toys (marketed under the name Trackmaster), which instantly gave Tri-ang Railways a die-cast clockwork 0-6-2 tank locomotive and two moulded plastic goods wagons. The tank locomotive, carrying the running number 69561, was a version of the N2 Tank so successfully modelled by Hornby-Dublo,

and was to be the only die-cast locomotive ever marketed by Rovex. The Tri-ang Railways version was slightly longer than the Hornby-Dublo version (150 mm to Hornby's 142 mm), lacked the red lining of the Hornby BR version, and early versions had 'British Railways' in yellow lettering on the tank sides, later replaced by the BR lion-and-wheel badge.

At the same time Rovex also produced its own tank locomotive from scratch, the 0-6-0 Jinty (officially the Fowler Class 3 Tank, or Class 3F).

Below The 1937–38 Book of Trains shows off the 'Princess Elizabeth'.

Richard Lines records that the original mould was used until 1975, during which time it was used to produce more than 800,000 body-casings. The Jinty was modelled on an LMS tank locomotive designed by Sir Henry Fowler and introduced in 1924. A massive 412 were built for shunting and light freight duties, and after nationalisation the Jinty saw service with British Rail until 1967. The Tri-ang version (the earliest of which had no running number) was in BR black livery. Later versions had the number 47606, and in 1970 a version was produced in its original LMS red livery with the number 7606 – the numbering system used after nationalisation

added 40,000 or 50,000 to former LMS locomotives, which meant that the LMS-liveried Jinty represented the same locomotive as the BR version.

The Tri-ang Jinty has proved so popular through the years, including an appearance as part of the Railway Children train set, that it has probably become more famous than the original on which it was based. Indeed, the model was so popular that within two years of the original Rovex tools wearing out, a new Jinty was launched with a completely retooled body. The new version appeared in 1978 and was a much more accurate representation of the Class 3F,

Right A boy plays with a model of the 'Princess Elizabeth' while a giant 'Flying Scotsman' looms in the background of the Gauge O leaflet, printed in July 1939.

having shed the dimensional errors of the original Rovex model.

At its launch in 1952, the new Tri-ang Railways was able to offer three locomotives (the N2, the Jinty and the original 'Princess Elizabeth') as well as a variety of rolling stock and lineside accessories. The system was an immediate success and within a few short years began to impinge on sales of Hornby-Dublo. Rovex Plastics Ltd, now renamed Rovex Scale Models Ltd, expanded so quickly that it soon outgrew its premises in the disused brewery in Richmond and moved in 1954 to a purpose-built factory in Margate which remains the headquarters of Hornby today, though not for much longer. By 1956, just four years after the launch of the new system, there was a choice of ten locomotives as well as a large range of rolling stock, trackside buildings and accessories – a phenomenally fast rate of production that was continued with the introduction of another four locomotives in the next two years, leading to the expansion of the factory in 1956 and again in 1959.

The rapid introduction of new locomotives continued into the 1960s with, among others, an L1 class 4-4-0 (as previously modelled by Hornby in Gauge 0) and the 4-6-2 'Britannia' in 1960; that old favourite the 'Lord of the Isles' and an EM2 class electric locomotive in 1961; an 0-4-0 diesel shunter in 1962; and a class B12 locomotive, Stephenson's 'Rocket' and the Caledonian Single in 1963.

The GWR 'Lord of the Isles' was built in 1851, a century before the Tri-ang Hornby model. It

was the first of the 4-2-2 Dean Singles, a class named after its designer, William Dean, and the fact that these locomotives had a single driving axle.

The 4-2-2 wheel arrangement arose because the excessive weight on the leading axle of the earlier 2-2-2 Great Western class had caused an axle to break, so it was strengthened by the addition of a second leading axle. The first GWR 4-2-2s were those of the Iron Duke class, followed just four years later by a larger version, of which 'Lord of the Isles' was the first. A total of 80 Dean Singles were built, including the 'Duke of Connaught', which took part in a record run of the Ocean Mail from Plymouth to Paddington on 9 May 1904.

Tri-ang Hornby's 'Lord of the Isles' was praised not just for the accuracy of the locomotive but also for the tender, whose spoked wheels added a great deal to the appearance of the whole. The single driving axle did not give much power to the model (as was the case with the real thing, which is why locomotives were later developed with more and more driving axles), but the ratio of the power of the motor to

Above The Jinty was the first locomotive to be designed by Tri-ang after Lines Bros had taken over Rovex.

Below The famous 'Lord of the Isles' arrived in 1961 and was the first classical locomotive to be modelled by Rovex – it was also the first to appear in anything other than contemporary BR livery.

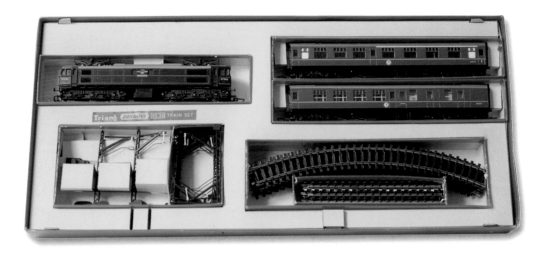

Right The EM2, Tri-ang's first main line electric locomotive, arrived in green livery in 1961 and bowed out in blue ten years later. An extensive range of catenary (overhead electric) equipment was produced in support of this and other similar models – a basic catenary system was supplied with this set.

the large size of the driving wheels made it one of the fastest locomotives in the Tri-ang Hornby range. As well as being the first of its class on the GWR, the 'Lord of the Isles' also marked a first for Tri-ang Hornby. Until the introduction of this model, Rovex had only made models of locomotives that were currently in existence, and only in their current liveries; the 'Lord of the Isles' was the first of several 'classical' models and was later joined by the Caledonian Single and Stephenson's 'Rocket', both in 1963.

The Caledonian Single used the same motor and much of the same tooling as the 'Lord of the Isles', and sold well because of its striking blue Caledonian Railway livery in a predominantly black and green range. The accompanying coaches were based on the framework of the new scale-length BR Mk 1 coaches but with specially-made side panels. The Caledonian Railway version was the only Scottish-owned 4-2-2, and was designed by Dugald Drummond and built as a one-off by Neilsons of Glasgow for the Edinburgh Exhibition of 1886. The model was an enormous critical success, leaving the *Model*

Railway News reviewer struggling for breath: 'Whoever would have thought it possible? A few years ago the mere idea would have seemed hopelessly wishful thinking. This most beautiful locomotive, Scottish, pre-grouping, not one of a large class, made by a proprietary firm at a toy price, leaves us gasping with delight.'

Meanwhile, the Co-Co EM2 Electric Locomotive, launched in the same year as 'Lord of the Isles', was available as a ready-to-run model representing No 27000 'Electra', and in kit form as No 27002 'Aurora' and 27006 'Pandora'. The EM2 had been introduced to BR in 1954 for the 1500-volt DC overhead power supply on the Manchester to Sheffield line, and the introduction of the model was intended to help boost sales of the Tri-ang Hornby overhead catenary system – the kits were supplied complete with a simple catenary comprising two masts and a length of overhead wire. Modelling the EM2 entailed developing a new motor bogie (known as the Mk VII), which proved to be very successful and paved the way for the introduction of other diesel and electric Co-Co locomotives.

As well as very quickly building up a large range of locomotives and rolling stock in the first decade of Tri-ang Railways, Rovex was also making technical innovations such as improving track and introducing smoke generators. The first smoke generator, introduced in 1961, was made by the German manufacturer Seuthe, but this was later replaced by Rovex's own 'Synchrosmoke' unit (patent no 961630), which emitted puffs of smoke that were synchronised with the revolutions of the driving wheels. Another Rovex invention was Magnadhesion, also first used in 1961. This was a system whereby magnets placed in the chassis of the locomotive magnetised the wheels in order to improve grip, but the system was later abandoned with the introduction of non-magnetic, nickel-silver track.

By the time of the 'amalgamation' with Hornby-Dublo, Tri-ang Railways was able to offer a choice of 24 locomotive types as compared with 15 shown in the final Hornby-Dublo catalogue, a measure of the speed of expansion and the productivity of Tri-ang Railways, which had been established just 12 years earlier. A genuine amalgamation would therefore have

provided a possible choice of 39 locomotives, a truly amazing total for one company. However, as Richard Lines pointed out in a 1966 interview for *Model Railway Constructor*, 'the price difficulty [with Hornby-Dublo] was largely due to the use of the more traditional materials and methods of manufacture and, consequently, the tooling was not generally as up-to-date and economic to use as comparable tooling on Tri-ang Railways'. In other words, Hornby-Dublo was simply too expensive to produce, and the writing was on the wall. This was borne out by the fact that of the seven Hornby-Dublo locomotives to appear in the amalgamation leaflet, three survived for only a year, appearing in 1965 price lists only, three more were deleted after appearing in the 1966 catalogue, and only one (the E3000/Class 81 Electric Pantograph Locomotive) made it into the Tri-ang Hornby range proper, and that after much modification. All subsequent introductions to the Tri-ang Hornby range (with the exception

Below The Old Smoky set, featuring a grimy locomotive' that produced real smoke – and a coach that had seats, always a popular element of real coaches.

of one tender chassis and one station building set) were developments of the existing Tri-ang Railways system rather than of the Hornby-Dublo system.

And so the names Tri-ang and Hornby were brought together, despite it being clear that the so-called 'amalgamation' had in fact been little more than a transfer of names from one range of products to another. Although the amalgamation took place in 1965 (15 months after the take-over), the Tri-ang catalogue for that year had been prepared the previous autumn and did not bear the Hornby name, so the first post-amalgamation items appeared under the name of Tri-ang Railways rather than Tri-ang Hornby. These included two new sets using existing Tri-ang locomotives: Old Smoky and Car-a-belle. The back page of the 1965 catalogue also made it clear just what a big player Tri-ang was in the toy

market, carrying the logos for four Tri-ang products at the top of the page, above an illustration showing how Tri-ang Railways, Minic Motorways, and buildings from Arkitex and Model-Land could be combined to create 'a world of miniature realism'.

Old Smoky pioneered the idea of 'weathered' trains, a concept reputedly suggested by the railway artist Terence Cuneo. Cuneo had been commissioned to 'weather' certain items (i.e. make them look dirty, as if they'd seen some action on a real railway) so that they could be photographed for a booklet brought out in 1962 to celebrate the tenth anniversary of Tri-ang Railways, which, perhaps not surprisingly, was entitled *Tri-ang Railways – The First Ten Years*. Ironically, the foreword was written by Dr Beeching, who was busy carving up the national rail network at the time. The weathered items looked so good in the

book that Tri-ang decided to introduce a weathered train set, known as Old Smoky, but this did not prove to be as great a success as had been hoped because, it seemed, buyers wanted their new toys to look new. The Old Smoky set comprised a weathered Deeley Class 3F locomotive and tender (already part of the Tri-ang range), together with two coaches.

Weathering made a comeback at the turn of the 21st century, much to the approval of *Railway Modeller*, which in March 2002 reported that: 'The Hornby factory weathering is actually very good, and this year they are doing more of it. Not only are most of us reluctant to try weathering a new, or even not so new, model it is doubtful whether many of us could achieve the quite subtle "in service" appearance . . . The weathered diesels are also very effective, and rightly look "oilier" than the steamers.'

The Car-a-Belle Set, which was also introduced in 1965, consisted of a Jinty tank locomotive and two Tierwag car transporters complete with scale model cars from Tri-ang's Minix range (Minix cars were built to the same scale as the railway system, and the name was chosen to link them to the Minic system in people's minds). British Rail operated six Tierwag car transporters on the national network, thereby providing Tri-ang with an ideal prototype on which to model a toy of immense play value – although in fact BR's limited stock meant that no-one could logically run more than three Car-a-Belle Sets on a single layout!

The 1966 catalogue at last carried the new Tri-ang Hornby name, and there are three candidates for the title of first Tri-ang Hornby locomotive. Many historians nominate the Co-Co English Electric Type 3, not to be confused with the Co-Co English Electric Type 5 'Deltic' modelled by Hornby-Dublo. The model of the Type 3 (later designated Class 37) appeared in 1966 and was the first new locomotive to be released after the announcement of the amalgamation – however, it had been planned, designed and tooled-up before that time and was therefore a thoroughbred

Tri-ang Railways locomotive in all respects apart from its catalogue date. Released shortly afterwards was the E3000/Class 81 Locomotive No E3001, the modified version of the Hornby-Dublo model representing No E3002. This is a far stronger contender for the title, in principle if not in release date, being the only Tri-ang Hornby locomotive that borrowed from both of the former systems. The outsider, which also appeared in the 1966 catalogue, is the 4-6-0 'Albert Hall' Steam Locomotive, announced and, in the main, developed after the change of name. And finally, the non-runner is the Hymek Diesel Hydraulic Locomotive, which had all the right qualifications (announced and developed after the amalgamation) and made it into

Above One of Peter Snow's favourites, 'Albert Hall' arrived in 1966 and was an attempt at levelling-up the balance of models between the regions – the swingometer showed that until now the Western Region had been all but ignored by Rovex.

Below In 1966 Rovex launched an all-weather gauge O system called Big Big, but it was not a big big success.

the 1966 catalogue but did not actually become available until 1967. And the winner of the title 'First Tri-ang Hornby Locomotive' is . . . a matter of opinion.

The 'Albert Hall' was a significant introduction to the Tri-ang Hornby range because hitherto (with the exception of the 'Lord of the Isles') Tri-ang Railways had virtually ignored the ex-GWR locomotives of BR's Western Region. 'Albert Hall' partially redressed the balance, and the choice of the Hall class to represent the GWR was based on several factors: Hornby-Dublo had already modelled the Castle class, and Graham Farish had modelled the King class, leaving the most obvious choices for Tri-ang Hornby as one of the Hall, Grange or Manor classes. Of these, a model of the Hall class would be able to make use of the B12 chassis already in production and so the Hall was chosen. It was an economic choice but, as a simple, rugged, unglamorous locomotive, perhaps not the best choice in terms of profile and popularity.

The Hall class on which the model was based was designed for the GWR by Charles Collett as a general purpose locomotive. The Halls were developments of George Jackson Churchward's earlier Saint class, and were introduced to the GWR in 1924 with 'St Martin', a modified Saint but technically the first of the new Hall class. The other locomotives of this class were built from scratch to a modified design and were introduced in two batches, one from 1928, and the so-called Modified Halls from 1944. The last was built in 1950, bringing the total number to 329, and the Halls were finally withdrawn from service in December 1963. The development of Halls from Saint class on the Great Western Railway was later reversed by Hornby Hobbies when the company modified the Hall class tools to produce a Saint for little extra cost during the 1980s, at a time when interest in the Hall class model was flagging.

The Tri-ang Hornby model initially appeared in BR green livery with the running number 4983, and was described in *Railway Modeller* as

'One of the most attractive locomotives to emerge from Margate. It is fully detailed, with many small, delightful touches . . . ' Later variations included a version released in 1970 in GWR livery, looking very similar to the BR green. This model came complete with alternative self-adhesive name and number plates, allowing buyers to rename their model as one of No 4916 'Crumlin Hall', No 6922 'Burton Hall' or No 5955 'Garth Hall' (a name which would probably look more at home on a football pitch or a country & western album cover than on a model railway).

TV presenter Peter Snow is an avid model railway enthusiast, and one of his favourite locomotives is his Tri-ang Hornby 'Albert Hall', which runs on an extensive three-circuit layout permanently set up in the attic. The attic conversion was specifically designed with trains in mind: 'We made sure we cut tunnels through the beams and I designed the internal furnishings of the room to make sure the railway worked around them. We had the railway shelf installed as part of the building work, so the train was always going to be an integral part of the conversion . . . In our last house the railway actually went through the bathroom, so you lay in the bath and the train would chunter past beyond the taps.'

As a travelling correspondent for the BBC, Peter Snow has bought goods wagons representing the rolling stock of each country he has visited, and he has a particular penchant for the Rhodesian railways. His enthusiasm for model railways is renowned not only within the family (his grandson yells 'Trains! Trains!' whenever he visits the house), but also among his colleagues. On leaving *Newsnight* he was presented with a black 4-6-2 with the name 'Newsnight' on the tender, a gift which he says

Above The Giraffe Car Set which later reappeared in the Battle Space range as the Sniper Car.

'never leaves the track'. Other Hornby stock includes an LNER 'Flying Scotsman', a Class 47 Diesel-Electric Inter-City and several super-detailed coaches and Pullman cars.

As well as the 'Albert Hall' and its accompanying new locomotives, a further significant addition to appear in this first Tri-ang Hornby catalogue was Battle Space. This was the beginning of what was to become a complete range of 'Rail based combat units' including, as advertised on the packaging, 'Tanks, guns, rockets that fire! Helicopters, planes, spy satellites that fly!'. The idea was developed in order to tap the popularity of earlier military models that had been part of the Tri-ang Railways system since a Rocket Launcher was introduced in 1957 – by the time of the amalgamation there were seven military wagons in the range, most of them in mid-green with NATO markings. The next step was to package the military hardware as a mini-brand in its own right, and Battle Space was afforded three pages of the 1966 catalogue. Most of the items previously available now appeared in

khaki, with fictitious markings to replace the NATO badges, while totally new items included a set of Battle Space Commandos and the Strike Force 10 Set, which comprised a standard Jinty in Battle Space khaki, a Catapult Plane Launching Car and an Assault Tank Transporter complete with tank.

The Catapult Plane Launching Car actually launched its cardboard plane from a wagon-mounted catapult, powered by a rubber band and triggered by a switch at the trackside. Such gimmicks may seem a somewhat frivolous distraction from the serious business of railway modelling, but it must be remembered that Rovex was primarily a toy manufacturer, recognition of which had enabled Tri-ang Railways to survive where Hornby-Dublo had failed to. Furthermore, 'gimmicks' with such enormous play value were the very thing that kept children interested in their railways, a point made in the *Model Railway Constructor* review of the Battle Space products: 'We are sure that these exciting operating accessories will keep many youngsters faithful to their railways long after the thrill of seeing a two coach express chasing its tail round an oval track has palled, and it must be faced that it is during this period that so many budding enthusiasts are lost to the hobby.'

With two of the three Battle Space pages given over to Battle, the third was devoted to Space, showing the new Satellite Set, which was made up of a red 0-4-0 Battle Space Diesel Shunter pulling a Spy Satellite Launching Car and a Radar Tracking Command Car. Again, the locomotive was the

Below Only one Hornby-Dublo locomotive was actually amalgamated into the Tri-ang Hornby system. After extensive modification the E3000 Class AL1/Class 81, originally released by Hornby as locomotive No E3002, was re-released by Tri-ang Hornby in 1966 as No E3001.

standard model in a new livery, and the wagons had working mechanical gizmos. The Spy Satellite Launch Car was similar to the earlier Tri-ang Railways Helicopter Launch Car, and used the same mechanism to spin the satellite as it was thrust into the air, while the radar dish on the Radar Tracking Car was turned by a drum connected to the wheel axles by a rubber band –

which was fine except that it meant the Tracking Car had to be on the move in order to track satellites, because the dish would not turn while it was stationary.

The other new development in 1966, though at a slight tangent to the development of the main Tri-ang Hornby system, was the launch of Tri-ang Big Big. This was a Gauge 0 system

Above The affectionately remembered Battle Space range of military models brought the world of toy soldiers to the model railway. The range included plenty of action gizmos such as satellite and plane launchers, the turbo car, and a sniper who ducked when he approached a low bridge (a variation of the earlier Tri-ang Giraffe car).

intended for children, and was designed to run inside the house as well as out in the garden, in all weathers. In an interview for *Model Railway Constructor* in February 1966 Richard Lines

Above More examples of the military models on offer from Battle Space.

Opposite page The cover of the 1969 catalogue.

commented that, 'Our new 0 Gauge train set is coming along very well and will be on the market very shortly. It is not, however, intended as a model railway so much as a toy train which has the great merit of being able to operate indoors and outdoors. We thoroughly enjoyed ourselves recently testing it under a shower!'

Whether parents approved of a toy that encouraged children to play outdoors while it was raining is not recorded – perhaps the idea was that the child would stay inside while the train went outside and got wet. The set came with more than 18 feet of plastic track that was capable of crossing obstacles such as door jambs leading to the garden, while the plastic-bodied locomotives were battery powered and therefore required no wiring. And one of the most useful features for a

set that was intended to run out into the garden was that it was fitted with a reversing lever so that the track did not have to be laid in a circuit. Sadly, Big Big did not prove profitable and was discontinued just six years later in 1972.

The big news of 1967 was the introduction of the 0-4-4 M7 Tank Locomotive, which featured on the cover of that year's catalogue in a painting by Terence Cuneo – Lines Bros made the most of their commission, also using the painting for a jigsaw marketed by Arrow Games, another member of the Lines Group. The British Railways M7 on which the model was based had originally been designed in 1896 by Dugald Drummond for the London & South Western Railway, where he had become chief mechanical engineer in 1895. (Drummond had previously been in charge at the Caledonian Railway, where he designed the Caledonian Single modelled in 1963 by Tri-ang Railways.) The LSWR had asked Drummond to find quotations for 25 new 0-4-4 Tank Locomotives, but all the quotations sought were too high and so the M7s were built to Drummond's design in the LSWR's own workshops at a cost of £1,445 each, entering service in 1897. They proved so successful that a total of 105 were eventually built, some as late as 1925, and 103 of them survived into the BR era. The last M7 was withdrawn from service in 1964, just three years before the Tri-ang Hornby model was launched and nearly 70 years after the introduction of the type to the rail network.

The advertising left users in no doubt as to the special features of the Tri-ang Hornby M7: 'Watch Out! Here comes the M7! Open the door (to see the tubes), Turn down the lights (to see the fire).' The M7 was actually introduced as a

PRICE 1/6

MODEL RAILWAYS & MOTOR RACING | EDITION 15.

IT 91

E3001

cheaper alternative to the larger 2-6-2 Standard Tank Locomotive, but the hinged smoke box door (revealing the flues within) and glowing fire box made it look like an exciting step forward. The pre-production model that was used in the advertisements carried the number 30021 but the production model, in BR black lined out with red and cream denoting passenger service, was No 30027 (the number of a locomotive built in 1904 and withdrawn in 1959). Later versions of the M7 included No 328 in light green Southern Railway livery and No 245 in the Southern Railway's earlier dark green livery.

In addition to the well-remembered M7, 1967 also saw a huge expansion of the popular Battle Space range, based on high sales the previous year. Fortunately for Rovex, most of the new additions were based on existing tooling to keep costs down, because the high sales were not repeated and only half of the new stocks were sold that year. Battle Space never recovered its popularity and was withdrawn during 1972, proving to have been a memorable but short-lived range.

Elements of the defunct Hornby-Dublo range were revived in 1967 when limited production of some former Hornby-Dublo items (as well as sales of remaining stock) was carried on by another member of the Lines Group, G & R Wrenn Ltd. Wrenn won the race to buy the Hornby-Dublo tools partly because Lines Bros did not want to sell them to a competitor and partly because the chairman, Walter Moray Lines, felt that it was important for Rovex to develop a first-class model range alongside the Tri-ang Hornby range of toy railways – acknowledgement of the quality of Hornby-Dublo if not its economic viability as a mainstream product. The ex-Dublo tools were used to produce the 'Cardiff Castle', the 8F Tender Locomotive and the 2-6-4 Class 4 Tank Locomotive for the launch of Tri-ang Wrenn in 1967. By 1969 these three locomotives had been joined by the 'Barnstaple' and the 'City of London'. All five were advertised in the 1969 Tri-ang Hornby catalogue as 'Heavy Die-cast Locomotives Built for Tri-ang Hornby by Wrenn'. In a small way Hornby-Dublo had

Below Second series station buildings, introduced in 1962.

been resurrected, but, significantly, the Wrenn locomotives did not sell as well as the main Tri-ang Hornby range – a belated answer to the vociferous complaints of Hornby-Dublo fans at the time of the take-over.

Lines Bros owned two-thirds of the shares in G & R Wrenn, and, after the collapse of the parent company in 1971, George Wrenn bought the Lines Bros shares back from the receiver, making Wrenn an independent company once again. Tri-ang Wrenn became Wrenn Railways, and continued to produce trains using the ex-Hornby-Dublo tools until George Wrenn retired and sold the company to Dapol in 1992.

The next new mainstream Tri-ang Hornby locomotive after the M7 was the celebrated Class A3 4-6-2 'Flying Scotsman' in 1968, which proved to be the company's most successful large

steam locomotive. BR's 'Flying Scotsman' was bought in 1963 by Alan Pegler, and news of the consequent preservation of this famous locomotive made it an obvious subject for model railway manufacturers – so obvious, in fact, that two manufacturers decided to produce it at the same time, and the race was on between Tri-ang Hornby and Trix to see who could get their model into the shops first. In the end, both managed to make their models available in August 1968: a tie on timing, but Tri-ang Hornby was to be the outright winner as far as sales were concerned.

Both companies initially produced two versions of the locomotive, one in BR Brunswick green livery bearing the number 60103 and one in LNER apple green with its original number, 4472; both were accurate reproductions of the 'Flying Scotsman' at different times in its career.

Above Hornby's most successful steam locomotive to date is 'Flying Scotsman', which first made its appearance in the Tri-ang Hornby range in 1968. It has subsequently been improved several times, resulting in 17 versions before the end of the century.

In December 1968 Trix also introduced a two-tender version of the LNER version, and in this race Hornby was 25 years behind, as it did not produce a two-tender version until 1993.

The 1968 Tri-ang Hornby advert explained the history of the locomotive (built in 1923 as a Gresley A1, rebuilt in 1947 as an A3 with the later additions of a double chimney and blastpipe), and announced: 'Now you can have superb models of this famous train, either as an LNER Locomotive and Tender which has Corridor Connections, or a BR version both in authentic liveries with Magnadhesion, Fire-box Glow and Cab detail, reproduced with the skill of the first name in Model Railways – Tri-ang Hornby.'

Until the 'Flying Scotsman' was produced, standard practice at Rovex had been for all locomotives (other than the historic models) to be issued in the current BR livery. The

'Flying Scotsman' bucked this trend because the British Railways locomotive had reverted to its LNER livery with its original number under preservation, and so there was great public interest in the original livery (in a sense, the LNER livery had become more 'current' than the BR livery). The LNER version was such a success that Rovex began to produce several other locomotives, coaches and wagons in their pre-nationalisation liveries. History was repeating itself in reverse: where Hornby-Dublo had produced locomotives and rolling stock in their current Group liveries and later had to update them to BR liveries, Tri-ang Hornby was producing them in BR liveries and later, by popular demand, releasing them in pre-nationalisation liveries – although a 1970 Tri-ang Hornby advertisement in *Model Railway Constructor* described them wrongly as pre-*Grouping* liveries.

Right In support of the new range of container wagons a Morris depot crane was introduced in 1969, capable of lifting containers between road and rail wagons.

After the introduction of only one new locomotive in 1967 (the M7), and one in 1968 (the 'Flying Scotsman'), there were none at all in 1969 – a sure sign that the general decline in sales of model railways had now hit Rovex, the company that by 1966 had managed to produce 28 new locomotives in its first 14 years. However, the slowing down of locomotive production was more than made up for in other areas. 1968 and 1969 saw the entire diesel and electric fleet become available in the new BR blue livery (complete with the new 'double arrow' logo), as well as the introduction of the first of the Mk 2 coaches and several revolutionary new goods wagons. The former Hornby-Dublo station buildings now became available in maroon with cream girders and grey platforms to conform with the rest of the Tri-ang Hornby station series, this being the only piece of true integration other than the Class 81 (E3000) Electric Locomotive. 1968 also saw the publication of the *Tri-ang Hornby Book of Trains*, a further reminder of the Hornby heritage, echoing the *Hornby Book of Trains* first published in 1925 to celebrate the centenary of the railways and help promote sales of the Gauge 0 Hornby Series.

The Mk 2 coaches, announced in 1968 but not available until the following year, were a reflection of the changes taking place on the national rail network, and took their place in the catalogue alongside the existing Mk 1 coaches and various classical and Pullman cars. Most of the existing vehicles were inherited from the Tri-ang Railways rolling stock, and the Mk 1 coaches available at the 'amalgamation' had been a composite, brake end and buffet car in maroon, green or maroon and cream, with sleeping and

full parcels brake cars available in maroon and cream only. The maroon and cream coaches were replaced from 1966 onwards by similar models in the new blue and grey livery recently introduced to British Rail, and the new Mk 2 coaches, when they arrived, also carried the new colour scheme, with the added bonus of carriage lighting powered from the track.

New goods wagons introduced in 1968 and 1969 included the 'Whisky' Bulk Grain Wagon, Slurry Tank Wagon, Cartic Car Carrier, and a container wagon with several variations of containerised loads. The popular bulk grain wagons were based on the 35-ton bulk grain hopper used on British Rail to transport malt barley grain from East Anglia to distilleries in Scotland, and carried advert boards for one of four whisky companies: Johnny Walker, Vat 69, Dewers or Haig. The wagons had been ordered

Above Two examples of Tri-ang Hornby's popular 'whisky' bulk grain wagons. These wagons were originally supplied by competitors Trix but very few were delivered and so Rovex tooled up its own model, which was slightly larger. Both are seen here, the Trix version advertising 'Haig' whisky and the Rovex version advertising 'Vat 69'.

Below The largest vehicle to be added to the Tri-ang Hornby range was the Cartic car carrier in 1969, which initially came with 16 individually packaged Minix cars.

Opposite page
Top The sleeping car, introduced to Tri-ang Railways in 1961, was the first Mk 1 coach to arrive, seen here alongside the same model made forty years later in 2001.
Bottom Mk 2 coaches were introduced in the classic blue and grey livery in 1968, and continued to be produced in those colours for many years. Some of the other liveries they carried are seen here. In 1998 they were replaced by the former Airfix Mk 2d coaches, one of which is seen here in Anglia livery.

from competitors Trix as part of a deal involving couplings, but Trix failed to deliver the required number of grain wagons and so Rovex tooled-up to make their own. These were produced with advert boards for Johnny Walker or Vat 69 only, and were slightly larger than the Trix version.

The container wagons provided another opportunity to introduce company logos to the model railway system (much as private owners' wagons had done before nationalisation), and the introduction of containerisation on the railway network was a blessing for all model railway manufacturers in that it allowed a large range of colourful models to be made for a comparatively low investment in new tools. There were only three units to make: the wagon itself, a 20-foot container, and a 30-foot container – thereafter it was simply a question of varying the liveries. (In fact, Rovex went the extra mile and produced an open container and a powder/liquid tank container as well as the two basic sizes of box container.)

The introduction of container traffic during the 1960s revolutionised shipping, road and rail transport worldwide, with new shipping companies coming together to form container

handling companies and to build new container ports specifically designed for the new traffic. The first commercial container-carrying train in Britain ran on 15 November 1965 between London and Glasgow, and Rovex was the first model railway manufacturer to follow suit with three 20-foot BR Freightliner containers on a flat-bed container wagon. This was followed by a change of livery to Freightliners Limited in 1970, and the subsequent introduction of containers in the company liveries of BP Chemicals, Harold Wood, Sainsbury's scotch beef, Containerway, Manchester Liners, Ford, Fyffe's bananas and Pickford's, as well as various liveries for foreign markets. The container revolution also initiated the launch of the Tri-ang Hornby Freightliner Depot Crane which could load and unload containers from road or rail wagons: the catalogue explained that it had three operating movements and could grasp or release a container, lift or lower it, and transfer it across the width of two tracks to or from a roadway.

It was a busy period for new goods wagons and accessories, because 1969 also saw the introduction of the Cartic Car Carrier. This was the longest wagon yet made by Rovex and it was

articulated, the two halves of the wagon sharing the centre bogie – a principle pioneered on the LNER by Nigel Gresley, and previously modelled by Hornby in both Gauge 0 and Dublo coaches. The Cartic was a great novelty because the two-storey car carrier was supplied with 16 Minix toy cars, although the number of cars was later reduced to 12. Whether the reduction was on the grounds of realism (the real thing only carried 12 cars) or for reasons of economy is open to question but, unusually, the two went together. *Model Railway Constructor* pointed out two inconsistencies with standard BR practice, complaining that the model rode the scale equivalent of 18 inches too high above the track, and that the Motorail insignia boards should have been on top rather than on the side of the upper deck.

1970 saw Tri-ang Hornby looking to the future and making long-term plans which, ironically, were to be carried out under new management – despite this long-term planning the parent company was to call in the receiver the following year. One example of Rovex's forward

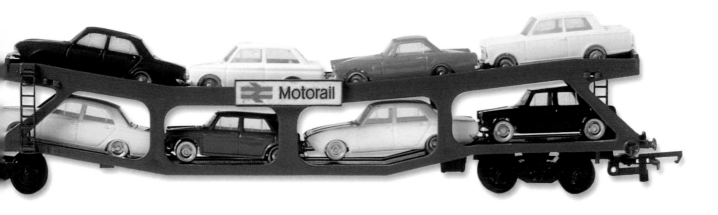

Above The Princess Coronation 'Duchess' class was introduced in 1977 as a replacement for the original Tri-ang Princess Coronation, whose tools were worn out after 25 years of use. The 'Duchess' had always been a popular model in the Hornby-Dublo system and made an obvious choice, appearing in many guises before being retooled in 2001. Seen here is the 'Duchess of Norfolk' in BR maroon livery.

thinking was a customer survey carried out in order to meet its customers' requirements more closely. A questionnaire was included with every copy of the catalogue, and by the end of the year more than 30,000 copies had been returned from countries as far afield as the Philippines, Czechoslovakia and Poland, including one from a US Senator. Suggestions for improvements included the introduction of scale wheels, better fishplates for connecting track, and heavier weights in rolling stock to make it ride more realistically. The survey also revealed that models of steam locomotives were more popular than diesel by a ratio of 5:1, and that pre-nationalisation liveries were preferred to BR liveries by a ratio of 2:1.

In fact, Tri-ang Hornby had read the market well and they were already in the process of introducing many of the improvements asked for. Even before all the questionnaires had been returned, System 6 track and fine-scale wheels were in production, while pre-nationalisation liveries were already becoming available following the success of the LNER version of the 'Flying Scotsman'. The existing Super 4 track was in the process of being upgraded, and so many improvements had been made to the proposed

new Series 5 track before it reached production that it eventually emerged under the name of System 6. This new track was a very successful compromise between the need for universality (i.e. that trains of many makes, including Hornby-Dublo and the older Tri-ang Railways, would run on it) and the desire for greater accuracy of scale, known as 'fine scale' rather than the previous 'coarse scale'.

The development of finer scale wheels went hand in hand with the track development, although in fact scale wheels had already been fitted to the Mk 2 coaches released the previous year. In 1970 these wheels, as well as being fitted to all new products, also became available in packs of four axles for customers wishing to update their older rolling stock. The new wheels were well received by the *Model Railway Constructor*, which described them as 'Very good and to an even finer scale than the old Hornby-Dublo coach wheels ... The introduction of these will stop many criticisms of Tri-ang Hornby wheels ... This is yet another sign that Tri-ang's are becoming more scale-minded.'

However, the limelight was stolen from these technical improvements by the launch of 1970's new locomotive, the streamlined LMS 4-6-2

Princess Coronation class. The Princess Coronation class was already familiar to Hornby-Dublo fans in the form of the 'Duchess of Atholl', which had been the first new Dublo locomotive to appear after World War II. However, the Tri-ang Hornby model looked very different from the 'Duchess of Atholl' as it represented the pre-war version of the class and so included the distinctive streamlined casing typical of the 1930s Princess Coronations. The class was designed by William Stanier as an enlarged and more powerful version of his Princess Royal class, and was built specifically to compete with Gresley's A4 during the 1930s for the title of fastest steam locomotive. No 6220 'Coronation' held this title for a short while, achieving 114 mph in June 1937 to beat the record set by Gresley's 'Silver Link' (modelled by Hornby in Gauge 0). It was to be a short reign, though, because the record was beaten the following year by Gresley's 'Mallard' which achieved 126 mph, a record for steam locomotives that has never been beaten since.

The streamlined casings of the first five Princess Coronations were painted blue and silver, as reproduced in the Tri-ang Hornby model, and in the mid-1930s this new class of locomotives hauled the Coronation Scot service between Euston and Glasgow, which for a while was the fastest scheduled railway service in Britain. There is some ambiguity surrounding the name of the class – officially the Princess Coronation class, they were referred to in the Rovex factory (and in some railway publications) as 'Coronations', because the Princess Royals were already known as 'Princesses'. To add to the confusion the later-built, non-streamlined versions of the class, though still officially called Princess Coronations, were popularly known as 'Duchesses' – even those that were named not after Duchesses but after British cities.

The Tri-ang Hornby Princess Coronation, which reached the shops in September 1970, was available with a choice of an additional three names and numbers. The model was supplied as the record-breaking No 6220 'Coronation', with self-adhesive name plates and number transfers providing three other choices for those who could

Below In line with real railway practice, Hornby started to introduce models of modern larger goods vehicles from 1979. These included vans, open wagons, steel carriers and hopper wagons.

be bothered to replace the factory-applied stickers and transfers with the new ones. The choices were No 6221 'Queen Elizabeth', No 6222 'Queen Mary' and No 6224 'Princess Alexandra'. For reasons of economy the locomotive used the same chassis as the 'Flying Scotsman', which made the Princess Coronation model slightly out of scale: it was 1 cm too short, with the bogie wheelbase 6 mm short and the bogie itself 4 mm too far back from the buffers. Another saving was made in the construction of the tender, which used the chassis of the former Hornby-Dublo model (borrowed back from Wrenn, which now owned the tools) – the mixed pedigree of the tender prompted *Railway Modeller* to claim that this was 'the first true Tri-ang Hornby model', although of course the E3000/Class 81 had been a similar hybrid.

Rovex had sacrificed scale accuracy for economy in the chassis of the Princess Coronations, a reminder that the company's prime purpose was still toy-making, despite the approving noises in the model railway press about fine-scale wheels and track. 1971 saw the introduction of two particular items of enormous appeal in the toy market as opposed to the modelling market, one of which was the introduction of exhaust steam sound, more onomatopaeically known as 'Chuff Chuff'. The device for making the chuff chuff noise was built into the tenders of selected models, and consisted of a projection from the rear axle of the tender which with each revolution of the wheels scraped against a rough surface similar to a piece of sandpaper.

The other item to appeal to this market was the Railway Children Set, also introduced in 1971. Rovex did not underestimate the importance of sets in gaining 'new recruits', and a themed set such as this one was ideal in that it might gain the interest of those not previously interested in model railways but had

Above Launched during the 'interregnum' between Lines Bros and DCM ownership, the Class 9F 'Evening Star' was a giant step forward for Rovex, being the most complicated locomotive the company had designed so far. It was also the first to have its motor in the tender.

After finishing the first five Princess Coronations in blue and silver, the LMS had built a further 15 (in two batches) in maroon and gold. Tri-ang Hornby followed suit the following year with No 6244 'King George VI', also supplied with stickers and transfers providing a choice of No 6221 'Queen Elizabeth' (thus now available in both liveries), No 6228 'Duchess of Rutland' and No 6241 'City of Edinburgh'.

been enthused by the film, which had been released the previous year. The screenplay was written by Lionel Jeffries, who is said to have been travelling to New York on the QE2 when his daughter told him that someone should make a film of the book she was reading – *The Railway Children* by E E Nesbit. EMI eventually accepted Jeffries' script, and the film, starring Jenny

Agutter, Dinah Sheridan and Bernard Cribbins, was shot on location mainly in Yorkshire, using the Keighley and Worth Valley Railway as the fictitious GN&SR (Great North & South Railway). Tri-ang Hornby's Railway train set was packaged with a scene from the film on the box lid, and contained the standard 0-6-0 Jinty Tank Engine in the ochre-yellow livery of the GN&SR, together with a maroon and white clerestory coach (i.e. with raised skylights) and a brown and yellow 'old time' coach. The set also contained a wayside station, power clip, uncoupling ramp and an oval of System 6 track.

For many the excitement of the silver screen was a mere distraction from what should have been the most compelling news of the year – the launch of the new locomotive for 1971, the revolutionary 2-10-0 Class 9F 'Evening Star'. But in the event, even this news was overshadowed by the fact that Lines Bros had gone into receivership, with the result that the 'Evening Star' was launched under the auspices of a company called Pocketmoney Toys Ltd. As with Meccano, the financial collapse of Lines Bros had come not as a result of any inferiority in the range

of products; indeed, the very quality of the product in both cases made it a shock that financial downfall should have occurred at all.

For Meccano Ltd, the problem had been complacency about competitors and a slowness to read the changes in the market (both leading to a loss of sales), combined with inherently uneconomical production methods. In the case of Lines Bros, the problem had been that profitable English companies within the Group had effectively been subsidising overseas subsidiaries that had been set up immediately after the war. Some of these companies had been set up to circumvent post-war trade barriers but, rather than taking the difficult decision to dispose of them when they became uneconomical, Lines Bros continued to support them. This was not helped by a general slump in the model railway market evidenced by the slowing rate of new locomotives being introduced at the end of the 1960s. The difference between the collapse of Meccano and that of Lines Bros, at least as far as the railway systems were concerned, was that while the changing market had rendered Hornby-Dublo obsolete as a mass-produced railway system, Tri-ang Hornby was a still-profitable part of a business empire that was collapsing around it. Accordingly, the receiver set up a new company, Pocketmoney Toys Ltd, in order to keep trading while a buyer was found.

It was in this 'interregnum', as Richard Lines refers to it, that the 'Evening Star' was launched. It is appropriate that No 92220 'Evening Star' should mark the end of this period in the history of the Hornby name, because this locomotive was the last steam locomotive to be made for British Rail, and marked the end of an era in its real as well as its model life. The Class 9F was designed for BR by Robert Riddles as a standard freight locomotive (although Riddles had left the Railway Executive before the class went into production in 1954), and the 'Evening Star' was unique in its class in that it was painted in BR's green passenger livery, lined out in orange, rather than the black freight livery. 'Evening Star' was named on 8 March 1960, and only four years later the withdrawals began, taking place from 1964 to 1968. Seven 9Fs have been preserved, including 'Evening Star' and one that was named 'Black Prince' after preservation, which was to enter the Hornby story at a later date.

For Tri-ang Hornby the 'Evening Star' was an extremely ambitious project, particularly at a time when the parent company was in financial trouble. The 2-10-0 wheel arrangement made it a technically difficult model to produce but, in going ahead, Rovex was to produce a model that would set the tone for all the company's future locomotives. 'Evening Star' created a new benchmark of quality in the same way that the 'Princess Elizabeth' had done for Gauge 0, and the 'Bristol Castle' had done for Dublo. The most revolutionary feature of the design was that the powerful Ring Field Motor was housed not in the body of the locomotive, as had previously been the case for all Rovex models, but in the tender, removing the need for any compromises in the design of the locomotive body in order to house the motor. The 9F received almost universal acclaim, reaching even the prevailing Continental high standards of modelling. *Railway Modeller* considered it 'one of the best scale models Tri-ang have yet produced', while *Model Railway Constructor* announced that it was 'a model of which we [the British] can be proud and it will stand comparison with the best . . . a near perfect 4 mm scale representation of the original . . . one of the finest proprietary models manufactured in the British Isles'.

High praise for the product of a company which, by the time the model became available, was in receivership. However, the reputation of Tri-ang Hornby was such that a buyer was soon found, and in January 1972 it was announced that toy manufacturer Dunbee-Combex-Marx (DCM) was to buy Rovex Tri-ang Ltd (as the company was then known) for £2,260,000. The Lines Bros trade-marks were sold separately, with the result that the name Tri-ang could no longer be used for the model railway system and, less than ten years after Tri-ang Railways had subsumed Hornby-Dublo, the system became known as 'Hornby Railways'.

DCM was so successful in reviving the fortunes of Rovex and Hornby Railways that within a year the factory had been extended and was working at full capacity trying to keep up with renewed demand. And, as in the days of Meccano management, Hornby under DCM was far from

Above The first locomotive to be
produced under DCM management
was the Black Five, which survived
with minor improvements for the next
29 years before being retooled in 2002.
The tooling for the original Black Five
(seen here) was then used to produce
Henry the Green Engine for the 'Thomas
the Tank Engine and Friends' series.

Below Railway purists saw red in 1973
when Hornby released a Hall class
locomotive named after the company
chairman Lord Westwood, and which
carried the company's telephone number
on its tender.

shy of publicity – the year after the change of management a pre-production model of a proposed new tender-powered 'Princess Elizabeth' was put through an endurance test and entered the *Guinness Book of Records* for bettering the feat performed by the Hornby-Dublo 'Cardiff Castle' 13 years earlier. (The proposed new 'Princess' was eventually abandoned in favour of an entirely new model of the Princess Coronation 'Duchess' class.) Richard Lines, writing in the *Hornby Book of Trains 25 Year Edition* describes how the 'Princess Elizabeth' completed 273.84 miles non-stop at Mevagissey Model Railway between 31 July and 8 August 1973, travelling nearly 124 miles further than the 'Cardiff Castle' had done.

The first new model locomotive to be produced under new management was the 4-6-0 Black Five class, based on a mixed traffic locomotive that had been built as the LMS's answer to the GWR's 4-6-0 Hall class (modelled earlier by Tri-ang Hornby). Designed by William Stanier, the Black Five entered service in 1934 and proved so successful that a staggering 842 were eventually built, more than three times the number which had been originally planned for; Black Five No 45110 had the honour of hauling the last steam train in operational service for BR. The Hornby Railways model proved to be extremely popular despite a number of discrepancies in the spacing and size of the wheels, the shape and size of the cylinders, and the chassis of the tender, which shared the same power unit as the 9F and was therefore too small for a correctly scaled model of the Black Five. The original model was supplied as unnamed locomotive No 45192, with stickers for No 45158 'Glasgow Yeomanry' and No 45156 'Ayrshire Yeomanry'. The tender accompanying

Hornby's later 1977 model of the Princess Coronation (Duchess) class was more suitable than the 9F tender, and was used for all variations of the Black Five from then on. Other versions of the Black Five included several in LMS black livery (including the same two named locomotives), one in LMS maroon, and one in a preserved green livery. The model was completely retooled ready for the 2002 season and three super-detailed versions were produced during that year.

As well as the Black Five, a memorable version of the Hall Class Locomotive was released in 1973. This was the 'Lord Westwood', a fictitious name for a completely unrealistic bright red Hall Class Locomotive (the Hall class was part of the GWR and would *never* have appeared on any railway in bright red). The departure from real railway practice infuriated the purists but brightened many a toyshop window and raised many a smile within Rovex and DCM. The locomotive was named after the DCM chairman Lord Westwood, and on the tender carried the company's telephone number, 25555. Originally it was to be a one-off, for a special presentation to Lord Westwood, who happened to wear an eye patch. Richard Lines remembers:

…somebody had the idea of making a little black patch to put over the spectacle plate [cab window] but he didn't spot it. He was very pleased, though, and when he took it home I think it was his son who burst out laughing, and then he saw the patch and he was tickled pink. But the thing was that I looked at this model and I thought, 'It looks absolutely cracking in bright red, so why don't we sell them?' We put it on the market the following year, this Hall class loco in bright red, and we sold huge quantities of them – much to the disgust of the purists.

A modified version of the earlier Tri-ang Railways L1 was also introduced in 1973, masquerading as a Class 2P 4-4-0. The L1 was a Southern Railway 4-4-0 Passenger Locomotive that had earlier appeared as one of the ground-breaking No 2 specials in the Gauge 0 Hornby Series, and in the Tri-ang Railways range in 1960. The Tri-ang Railways model was now modified to represent the LMS Class 2P Locomotive, a class that was later produced in a super-detailed scale version in 1999. Apart from this modified version of an earlier model, it was to be a relatively long

wait between the launch of the endurance-record-breaking Black Five in 1973 and the next completely new locomotive, the Class 47 Co-Co Diesel, in 1975. The Class 47 was introduced to British Railways in 1961/62 after a number of different diesel types had been tried: this particular one was based on a locomotive built in Switzerland for the Romanian State Railways (the Class 060DA). The bodywork was modified and the power of the engine was uprated for BR, after which a total of 512 Class 47s entered service, some of them still in operation in the 21st century.

Above Back on the gravy train – perennial favourite the Palethorpe's Sausages van was based on a type of van that once ran on the GWR, and was already familiar to fans of Hornby Gauge 0 from a model produced by Meccano in 1938. The Hornby Railways version seen here is an example of the only six-wheeled wagon to be produced at Margate, and was available in two liveries in 1976.

The Hornby model was referred to at planning meetings as 'Falcon' after BR's experimental locomotive, although it was eventually released as unnamed locomotive No D1738. Later named versions included No 47712 'Lady Diana Spencer' (introduced in 1981, the year that an estimated 700 million people worldwide watched the 'wedding of the century'), and No 47451 'The Queen Mother', keeping good company with No D1670 'Mammoth' and No 47480 'Robin Hood', among others. As with the Black Five, the motor bogie that was initially used for the Class 47 was the wrong size to be a correctly scaled model, and this was later changed for the drive mechanism used in the 9F tender, which was the correct size. BR's Class 47s came to be widely used by Railfreight

and the Freightliner Company, and later still by Virgin Trains, in all of which Hornby followed suit, producing Class 47s in a variety of colours and liveries.

In April 1976 Rovex Models & Hobbies Ltd became Hornby Hobbies Ltd, which further consolidated the link between the Hornby name and the former Tri-ang Railways system – the entire system was now marketed *and* manufactured under the name Hornby. While the company was riding high from the change of name and management (a new managing director had been appointed to Hornby Hobbies, which had now become an independent division of DCM), Hornby's position in the marketplace had come under threat. This threat came from two new competitors, both of which had recognised a gap

Right The Hull & Barnsley Railway van, introduced in 1972, carried many liveries over the years but none more appropriate than Yorkshire Pudding Co. in 1982.

in the market for ready-to-run model railways with greater accuracy and better finish. The new ranges in question were Mainline (manufactured by Palitoy) and Airfix. Hornby was concerned that with three companies competing at the top of the market the lower end would possibly be exposed to competition from elsewhere. However, the fact that the systems of both rival companies were launched at almost the same time, and that both had delivery problems from their Chinese suppliers, played directly into the hands of Hornby. Customers and retailers waiting for delayed products from Mainline and Airfix turned to Hornby instead, which resulted in extremely good business for Hornby in 1976 and 1977.

During these two years, Hornby introduced a Class J83 Tank Locomotive, a Class N15 'King Arthur' 0-4-0, a non-streamlined Princess Coronation (Duchess) Class 4-6-2, a Class 25 Bo-Bo Diesel and a Class 43 HST, more popularly known as the 'Inter-City 125'. The Duchess arrived in 1977 in the form of No 6233 'Duchess of Sutherland' in LMS maroon livery, recalling the Hornby-Dublo 'Duchess of Atholl'. Meccano Ltd had produced four versions of its Duchess in the Hornby-Dublo range, and Wrenn went on to produce a further 18 versions after acquiring the tools. The Duchess modelled by Hornby Hobbies in 1977 was completely unrelated to the Dublo/Wrenn models, being manufactured from a new set of tools that was

used to model 18 members of the class for Hornby Railways before being replaced in 2002 with a completely new, super-detailed set.

It is interesting to note that, rather than modelling a Duchess back in 1950, Rovex had modelled a Princess in order not to duplicate the Duchess in the Hornby-Dublo range. The Princess tooling went on to produce 779,695 models before it wore out in the 1970s and the model was withdrawn. Hornby Hobbies considered replacing the Princess with a retooled version but decided on the Duchess instead, which duly appeared in 1977. Later, in 1984, a new scale-length version of the Princess was produced, and this was itself updated to super-

Above The High-Speed Train, or Inter-City 125, was one of the few diesel-electrics to possess real character, and has proved a particularly popular model with Hornby fans. It appeared in a number of different liveries before once again being released in blue and grey in 2002.

detail standard in 2001, with the result that Hornby now had very high-quality models of all three LMS Pacifics – the Princess, the Coronation and the Duchess.

The Class 43 HST (high-speed train), launched in the same year as the 'Duchess', has proved to be one of Hornby's most popular models, despite having to compete with a similar model representing a later version of the Type 43, produced by competitors Lima. The British Railways high-speed train is renowned as one of the most successful and influential designs ever to run in the UK, running at up to 125 mph on the existing rail network (hence the popular name 'Inter-City 125'). BR introduced a prototype in 1972, which broke several world speed records for diesel traction, and the HST went into full service on the Western Region main line in October 1976. Technically speaking, the HST was not hauled by a locomotive: it was a self-propelled unit with a 'power car' at each end, coupled to a number of Mk 3 coaches (usually seven or eight).

Hornby brought out its model in 1977, within a year of the HST going into service, and it was later described by S W Stevens-Stratten in the *Hornby Book of Trains 25 Year Edition*:

The power cars are exact scale models of the prototypes and one is fitted with the Silver Seal Ringfield motor unit and both cars have headlights which illuminate in the direction of travel when the power is switched on. A representation of the cab interior can be seen through the windows and the body detail, colouring and Western Region lettering are all authentic . . . Great realism can be obtained in the operation of the layout if the HST train [sic] is allowed to pass several stations, slightly slowing down as it passes some and then quickly speeding up again

. . . You may wish to run the HST for several circuits before stopping, to simulate the longer distances incurred in reality.

1977 was also the year of the Queen's Silver Jubilee, which was celebrated by Hornby in grand style with the delivery of a billboard-sized congratulatory card to Buckingham Palace, and the production of two special Silver Jubilee Sets. One was the 'Silver Jubilee Pullman Set', comprising the 'Albert Hall' Locomotive, four first-class Pullman parlour cars, a battery controller, tunnel, island station, level crossing, two junction signals, a large oval of track, an uncoupling ramp and a power clip. The other was the 'Silver Jubilee Freight Set', which was made up of a Class 47 diesel locomotive, eight wagons, a battery controller, tunnel, island station, level crossing, a large oval of track, two sidings with buffer stops, two uncoupling ramps and a power clip. The wagons were a Southern Region sheep wagon, a Hull & Barnsley 'Prime Pork' refrigerated van, a blue 'Kelloggs' van, a 'Norstand' mineral wagon, a 'Bestwood' five-plank open wagon, a 'Minera' lime wagon and a short grey LNER brake van.

1976 and 1977 had been bumper years for Hornby, and the two-year gap between Airfix and Mainline exhibiting their pre-production models and actually getting them into the shops gave Hornby plenty of time to move up-market and meet the challenge with finely-detailed models of its own. By 1978, when Airfix and Mainline were beginning to have an impact, Hornby was already well ahead of the game, with an impressive-looking new-style catalogue showing a number of new locomotives including the Holden tank, Class 29 Bo-Bo Diesel and King Class 4-6-0, as well as a new range of regional coaches and a third generation of station buildings.

Above Regional coaches were introduced in 1977 and, while not scale models, they were convincingly designed in the styles of Collett (GWR), Maunsell (SR), Stanier (LMS) and Gresley (LNER). Here is a representative cross-section of the many versions made over the next 25 years.

The 0-4-0 Class 101 Holden Tank Locomotive was based on a locomotive designed for the GWR by James Holden, who developed a number of oil-fired steam locomotives using a by-product of the oil-gas used for carriage lighting. The Class 101 was one of a kind, built in 1902 as a solitary experimental oil-burner – the experiment proved unsuccessful and the locomotive was subsequently converted to coal in 1905. It was built at Swindon and never left the site, being used as a works shunter until it was withdrawn from service in 1911. The reason that such an obscure locomotive came to be modelled by Hornby was that the company was looking for a new 0-4-0 for its Starter Sets, and Richard Lines saw the Holden while looking through a set of drawings of possible subjects to model. He chose this locomotive over the other candidates because, apart from having the required wheelbase, 'It seemed a nice subject, looking typically GWR and having a copper chimney cap.'The Hornby model was produced in GWR green livery and represented the Holden after conversion to coal. Later versions appeared in a variety of bright colours and whimsical liveries, including yellow with Colman's livery, white with Ford logo, and another in GWR green celebrating the 150th anniversary of the GWR in 1985.

The King class (also known as the Class 6000 or 60XX) was another GWR steam locomotive introduced in the same year as the Holden tank. The Kings were designed by Charles Collett and introduced in 1927 as a development of the earlier Castle class, and were the most powerful of the British 4-6-0s in terms of tractive force. All 30 locomotives of the class were built with single chimneys that were upgraded to double chimneys during the 1950s, and all had been withdrawn from regular service by 1962.The Hornby model first appeared as No 6024 'King Edward I' in GWR green, with later versions representing several other members of the class in GWR green, BR green and BR blue.

As well as new locomotives, 1978 was also notable for the introduction of so-called regional coaches ('pre-nationalisation coaches' would have been a more accurate name). With many Hornby locomotive models by then in pre-nationalisation liveries it was important that some believable coaches were produced to go with them, and in 1978 four sets of 'regional' coaches were launched in the approximate liveries of the four Groups. (Before this time the only pre-nationalisation coaches had been unconvincingly modified versions of the BR Mk1 and Caledonian coaches.) Although not

Above The Holden tank locomotive, introduced in 1977, was based on an experimental locomotive that was a one-off – yet Hornby managed to produce more than 20 versions in a variety of liveries! Here we see the version produced to commemorate the 150th anniversary of the GWR in 1985.

strictly based on actual railway rolling stock, the new range succeeded in conveying the character of the four major companies, and are generally referred to after the engineer whose style was represented. Thus for the LMS there are three Stanier-type coaches, including a travelling post office; for the GWR there are three Collett-style coaches, including a restaurant car; for the LNER there are three Gresley-style coaches, including a sleeping car; and for the SR there are two coaches in the style of Maunsell. An old Tri-ang model of a bogie utility van was then reintroduced using the original tooling to provide the Southern with a third vehicle. As well as being produced in their original Group liveries, all except for the Colletts were later released in BR regional liveries.

Yet again financial problems were on the horizon for Hornby's parent company, but in the meantime Hornby Hobbies was trading healthily and continuing to introduce new models: five new locomotives in 1979, including the Gresley A4, Class E2 Tank and Patriot Class 4-6-0, with another four in 1980, including the Class 4P

Tank, B17 Tender Locomotive and Class 370 APT – the infamous 'tilting train'.

Gresley's A4 was another locomotive that had previously been modelled by Hornby in both Gauge 0 and Dublo. The first four LNER A4s were produced in silver-grey and were used to haul the Silver Jubilee Express service inaugurated in 1935, the year of George V's Silver Jubilee. One of these four, No 2509 'Silver Link', had appeared as part of Hornby's Gauge 0 'No 0 Silver Jubilee Clockwork Train Set'. The next nine A4s left the factory in standard LNER green livery, while those that were assigned to the Coronation and West Riding Express services appeared in 'garter blue', as represented in the Hornby-Dublo model of No 4498 'Sir Nigel Gresley'. From 1937 onwards all A4s adopted the garter blue livery and then went through several changes with wartime black livery, a post-war return to garter blue, an experimental dark blue immediately after nationalisation, and finally BR Brunswick green with black and orange lining – all of which gave Hornby plenty of options to choose from. Between the release of No 60022 'Mallard' in BR green livery during 1979 and No 60017 'Silver Fox' in 2002, the Hornby A4 appeared in no fewer than 40 variations, including examples of all the various colours listed above – the largest collection of A4s to be produced by a single manufacturer.

In contrast there were relatively few variations of the Class E2 Tank Locomotive, released the same year as the A4. One of the reasons for the small number of variations was that within a decade of its introduction the tools were to be converted to make Thomas the Tank Engine, which meant that no further versions of the E2 tank could be made. Hornby's E2 was modelled on a class of ten tank locomotives designed by L B Billinton and built between 1913 and 1916 for the

Below Yesterday's World – Stephenson's 'Rocket' is probably the most famous and instantly recognisable locomotive in the world. Hornby's 3 ½" gauge live steam model of the 'Rocket' was produced in 1979, the 150th anniversary of the success of the original 'Rocket' at the Rainhill Trials. The development of the Hornby model was filmed by the BBC for the science programme Tomorrow's World.

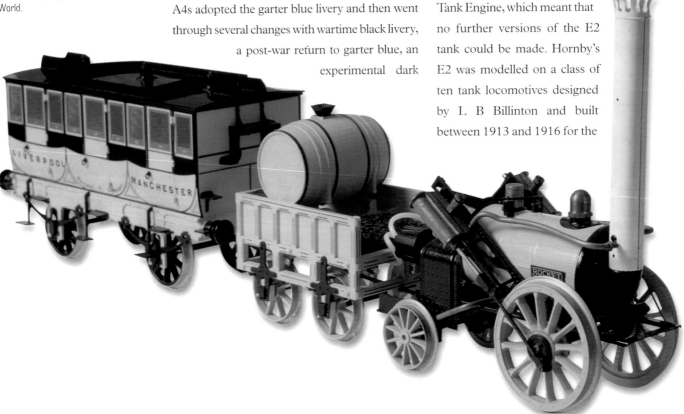

London, Brighton & South Coast Railway, and the model first appeared in the 'Marsh umber' livery of the LBSC. The LBSC became part of the Southern Railway at the 1923 Grouping, and this was one of the reasons why Hornby chose to model this particular type – until 1979 Hornby had good models of 0-6-0 tanks representing the LNER, GWR and LMS, but nothing for the Southern. The LBSC livery survived until 1928, five years after the Grouping, so it had the dual advantage of pleasing SR fans while providing a new colour variation for everyone else (new colours had often proved to be a good selling point). The model, which appeared as locomotive No 100, used the Jinty chassis and was detailed with 'delicate double lining and wire handrails'. The only later variations were No 104 in Southern olive green livery (with alternative numbers) and No 103 in Southern black livery, a rare version much sought by collectors.

For those who had been adding even a fraction of the growing number of locomotives to their system, control was of the essence, and in 1979 Hornby released a revolutionary new control system known as Zero 1. The big difference between Zero 1 and earlier control systems was that the locomotives were controlled

by a microchip within the locomotive rather than by the current passing through the track, which meant that in theory up to 16 locomotives could be independently controlled, even when they were in the same track section. The system was described by J M Kedge in *The Hornby Book of Trains 25 Year Edition*:

Hornby's latest successful investment could well mark the biggest change in model railways since the introduction of two-rail electric systems. Hornby's 'Zero 1' is a complete control system based on the latest micro electronic technology and it enables the user to control not only locos but also to operate points and other electrical accessories. All this with just two wires from the controller to the track.

Phase 1 of the system, available in the late Autumn of 1979, offers complete locomotive control. Phase 2, planned for introduction in early 1980, brings control of points, colour lights, signals and other operating accessories.

First of all the system was very complicated to use, and in practice most people could not control any more than four locomotives, only a

Above The name 'King George V' had been associated with Hornby trains since the first tinprinted trains of 1920. The association was revived in 1985 when the Hornby's King class model, first introduced in 1978, was released as 'King George V' in GWR green livery. Pictured is a later example of 'King George V' in BR express blue livery (released 1996).

Below The Rev Awdrey repainted his Hornby E2 tank locomotive to become Thomas the Tank Engine on his own model railway. Hornby followed suit in 1985, using the tools of the E2 to create Thomas for the commercial market. Pictured is the E2 as first released by Hornby in 1979 in the 'Marsh umber' livery of the LBSC, which became part of the Southern Railway at the 1923 Grouping.

Inter-City 125 from
York to London
2 hrs 4 mins

Inter-City 125 from
Leeds to London
2 hrs 9 mins

Above BR exhibition at York April 1979 to celebrate full service of the High-Speed Train on the East Coast Main Line.

quarter of the 16 advertised. Many units were returned to Hornby during the first year, not because they were faulty but because users simply couldn't understand how to use them. However, the system was refined and ultimately proved to be very popular.

The following year saw the introduction of another tank locomotive, the 2-6-4 Class 4P. This was a late replacement for the Class 3 2-6-2

Tank Locomotive that was discontinued in 1973, leaving Hornby with no large tank locomotive in the range. The 4P was a good choice because it originated before nationalisation, allowing for variations in the livery of the model, which Hornby had by now recognised as a good way of maximising sales. Designed for the LMS by Sir Henry Fowler and introduced in 1927, the 4P was designed for fast suburban passenger traffic,

but during World War II proved perfectly capable of hauling heavy express trains. The first Hornby model represented No 2300 in LMS maroon, with later versions in LMS maroon with various numbers, LMS black and BR black. The model was upgraded to super-detail standard in 2002.

The 4P was joined in the 1980 catalogue by the 4-6-0 Class B17, also known as the Sandringham class and, informally, as the 'Footballer'. The B17 was of a totally different design to earlier Hornby models – instead of being a single moulding, the body was made up of several individually moulded components, which allowed Hornby to include detail in places

where it had not previously been possible, such as under the boiler. The B17 was another Gresley express passenger locomotive, introduced to the LNER in 1928 and named after towns and mansions in East Anglia, with later-built examples named after football teams. Interestingly, all the variations produced by Hornby were named after football teams rather than towns, revealing something about the company's target market. The first Hornby B17 to appear was No 2862 'Manchester United' in LNER green, with alternative stickers for

Above The Class B17, aka the 'Footballer'. Introduced in 1980, this was a good choice of subject in terms of marketing, with many of the big name football clubs to choose from. Pictured is 'Doncaster Rovers', released in 1998.

Below and next page Hornby was so far ahead of the game with its advanced passenger train (APT) that the model was the nearest most people got to seeing the so-called 'tilting train' in action – the project to build the real thing was abandoned as a failure in 1986, six years after the Hornby version arrived in the shops.

No 2864 'Liverpool', No 2848 'Arsenal' and No 2866 'Nottingham Forest'.

Among the last locomotives of another Hornby era was the Class 370 APT (advanced passenger train), more popularly known as the 'tilting train'. The infamous 'tilting train' never actually made it into full service with BR, being superseded by other high-speed trains before its many technical problems had been ironed out. The project was initiated because of the need for shorter journey times and, knowing that the British government would not invest in new track, as had been the case in France and Japan, the only answer was to produce a 'tilting train' that could take the curves of Britain's existing lines at a greater speed. In this the prototype APT succeeded, improving speeds on bends by up to 40 per cent and with a top speed on the straight of 160 mph. However, despite this success the train proved unreliable, suffering from numerous problems relating to the hydrokinetic braking system, the tilt mechanism and the gearboxes. Furthermore, the tilting mechanism was said, perhaps not surprisingly, to increase travel sickness. The entire project was abandoned in

1986, by which time BR had commissioned the InterCity 225 and embarked on a programme of track modernisation that included easing the curvature of the main lines.

But by the time BR abandoned the APT, Hornby's model had been in the shops for six years! The idea of Hornby modelling the APT is thought to have originated with Richard Lines, who always kept an eye on developments on the real railways when considering subjects to model. He and other members of the Hornby design team got a ride on the prototype APT as part of their research but, having travelled to Preston to join it, they only managed to travel as far as Crewe before they had to stop because the overhead wires further south had been brought down by snow. Great secrecy surrounded the Hornby APT while it was in development, to the extent that even in the minutes of the Development Committee it was referred to as the 'Ramsgate Project'. The model appeared as No 370 001/2 'City of Derby' only, in grey livery, although for some unknown reason there were two variations of this locomotive, one with an all-yellow cab front and one with a yellow and black cab front.

After producing nine new Hornby Railways locomotives in two years, the financial collapse of DCM in 1980 could be seen as being the opposite of the demise of Dublo – ending not with a whimper but with a bang. Except that the end of DCM was not the end of Hornby Railways. Once again the Hornby name rose from the metaphorical ashes, and Hornby Railways remained at the forefront of the market the following year, 1981, designated by the company as The Year of the Loco.

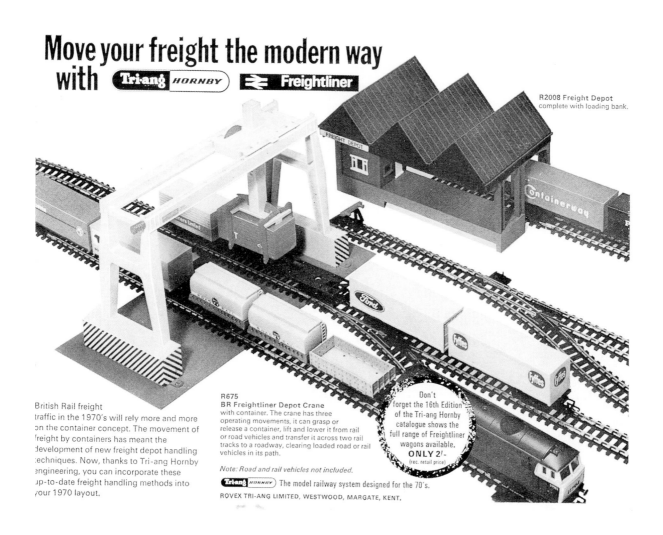

Move your freight the modern way
with Tri-ang HORNBY ⟩ ⟨ Freightliner

R2008 Freight Depot complete with loading bank.

British Rail freight traffic in the 1970's will rely more and more on the container concept. The movement of freight by containers has meant the development of new freight depot handling techniques. Now, thanks to Tri-ang Hornby engineering, you can incorporate these up-to-date freight handling methods into your 1970 layout.

R675
BR Freightliner Depot Crane
with container. The crane has three operating movements, it can grasp or release a container, lift and lower it from rail or road vehicles and transfer it across two rail tracks to a roadway, clearing loaded road or rail vehicles in its path.

Note: Road and rail vehicles not included.

Tri-ang HORNBY ⟩ The model railway system designed for the 70's.

ROVEX TRI-ANG LIMITED, WESTWOOD, MARGATE, KENT.

Don't forget the 16th Edition of the Tri-ang Hornby catalogue shows the full range of Freightliner wagons available.
ONLY 2/-
(rec. retail price)

From the
Year of the
Locomotive
to the Virtual
Railway

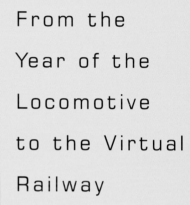

Below and page 140 No 2 Specials revisited – among the new models released in 1981, 'The Year of the Locomotive', were four 4-4-0 tender locomotives which had previously been modelled in Gauge 0, three of them as No 2 Specials. The gang of four included the LNER Shire/Hunt class (represented here by a 1983 model of 'Yorkshire' in BR black), and the Southern Railway Schools class which had appeared as a No 4 locomotive (represented here by a 1986 model of 'Eton'). Page 140 shows the GWR County class and the LMS Compound.

Hornby Railways' publicity described 1981 as 'The Year of the Locomotive': an apt title for a year that saw the addition of no less than seven completely new locomotives to the range, as well as nine new variations of existing models. It was a triumphant display of confidence for a brand whose second parent company in ten years had gone into liquidation the previous year – and this confidence was not just hollow bravado. Hornby's management had demonstrated that it was quite prepared to put its money (and other people's) where its mouth was, having bought Hornby Hobbies from the receivers with the aid of venture capital. The newly created parent company was named Wiltminster Ltd, and Hornby Hobbies Ltd became a wholly owned subsidiary, manufacturing model railways which continued to be marketed under the name Hornby Railways.

The new locomotives that appeared in the 'Year of the Locomotive' catalogue included the LMS Compound, the LNER Shire/Hunt class and the GWR Churchward County class – all previously modelled as No 2 Specials in the Gauge 0 Hornby Series in 1929, when Meccano's

publicity had announced that 'this year Hornby Trains are better than ever'. The departure from the precedent set by Gauge 0 was that the Southern Railway was represented not by the L1 as in 1929 but by the Schools class, which had been introduced to Gauge 0 in 1937 as a No 4 locomotive. This 'gang of four' was joined in the same year by the Class 2721 0-6-0 Open Cab Pannier Tank, Class J13/J52 0-6-0 Tank and the Class 86 Electric.

More than half a century earlier four 4-4-0s had been chosen by Meccano as suitable locomotives to model because they represented the big four companies and because they shared not only a common wheel arrangement but also a number of other features, allowing Meccano to use several components in more than one model. Some of these similarities were put to good use again in 1981 but came under closer scrutiny this time, drawing some criticism in an age when greater accuracy was expected. The most obvious discrepancies were in the model of the Midland Compound, which was built according to the dimensions of the Schools class model. This meant that, among other things, the coupled driving wheels of the Compound were the wrong size and too far apart, and that the leading bogie wheels were not large enough.

Hornby's model of the Compound first appeared as Locomotive No 1000 in LMS maroon, representing the first of the real Compounds to have been built, but in its post-Grouping livery rather than its original Midland

Railway livery. Interestingly, the number 1000 was initially carried by the sixth Compound to be built, and the number was only given to the first of the class after a later batch had been built and the entire class renumbered. The Compound had originally been designed for the Midland Railway (pre-Grouping) by Samuel Johnson, and the first of them took the number 2631 when it went into service in 1902. Four more Johnson Compounds followed in 1903 and proved so successful that Johnson's successor Richard Deeley built 40 more slightly modified Compounds, the first 30 of which were numbered 1000 to 1029. As explained, this numbering was later adjusted to recognise Johnson's Compounds as the first of their class, Johnson's taking the numbers 1000 to 1004 while Deeley's became 1005 to 1034. (The last Deeley batch was then numbered 1035 to 1044 as it was built.)

After the absorption of the Midland Railway into the LMS at the 1923 Grouping, a further 195 Compounds were built for the LMS,

Johnson's design having been further modified by Sir Henry Fowler. Later versions of the Hornby model included No 1000 in its original red Midland Railway livery (in which livery this locomotive has been preserved at the National Railway Museum in York), and No 41043 in BR black. The BR version was given the short Fowler-style tender that had been modelled to accompany Hornby's Patriot class locomotive.

The Southern Railway Schools class, which shared a chassis with the Compound, is considered to be one of Hornby's best models of that period, and was produced in far more variations than any of the other 4-4-0s introduced in 1981. However, this popular model was nearly not made at all, having been abandoned in 1979 when Hornby discovered that Airfix was also developing a Schools class model. In the event Airfix folded in 1981 and Hornby went ahead with its model, first producing No 910 'Stowe' in SR malachite green. Because of its short name, 'Stowe' was fitted with a short nameplate that later had to be enlarged to allow for models of locomotives with longer names. In all, Hornby produced 18 versions of the Schools class in four different Southern and BR liveries.

Another discrepancy crept in by way of Hornby's model of the Shire/Hunt class (officially designated Class D49) because Hornby used the same tools to produce both variations of the original locomotives. The first 34 LNER D49s had Walschaert's outside valve gear and were named after shires, hence the popular name of the class. From 1932 to 1935 the last 40 D49s were built with rotary camshaft gear and named after famous fox-hunting packs. (Before the adoption of hunt names for the rotary camshaft variations, two such examples had been built and named after shires: these were later renamed after hunts.) The first Hornby model represented Shire

Of the 1981 4-4-0s, history repeated itself most closely with the Churchward County, which appeared as No 3821 'County of Bedford' in GWR green, as it had done in 1929. Unlike Meccano, Hornby had learnt that variations on a theme boosted sales, and later released four other variations of the model. However, it was Hobson's choice of livery because all of the real Churchward Counties had been withdrawn from service by 1933 and therefore never appeared on the railways in BR livery, so all the Hornby variations appeared in GWR green. On the Great Western Railway the Churchward County (so named to distinguish it from the later 4-6-0 Hawksworth County) had been eclipsed by the City class, but the reverse was true on Hornby Railways – later in the 1980s Hornby made a sample model of the 'City of Truro' but decided

Below Hornby again beat BR off the mark by releasing the Class 58 diesel in 1982 before the real locomotive emerged from the paint shops. Here we see the first named model, 'Bassetlaw' (1988), in Railfreight red line grey livery.

locomotive No 2753 'Cheshire', one of the earlier D49s, but the same tools with the same valve gear were used for models of Hunt locomotives No 359 'The Fitzwilliam', No 222 'The Berkeley', No 62750 'The Pytchley' and No 62758 'The Cattistock'. In 1983 Hornby produced No 62700 'Yorkshire', the same locomotive that had appeared as a Gauge 0 No 2 Special, but this time in BR black livery where in Gauge 0 it had been in LNER green.

not to put it into production because it looked too much like the Churchward County.

The offerings in 1981 had lived up to Hornby's billing as the Year of the Locomotive, but unfortunately model railways were a low priority for the new managing director of Hornby Hobbies, who had taken over during that same year. The rate of introduction of new locomotives was almost immediately curtailed in favour of out-and-out toys such as Pound Puppies, Gro

Above 1982 saw the release of an excellent model of a Class 110 diesel multiple unit (DMU), which appeared in various BR liveries including the classic blue and grey, seen here.

Below The original clerestory roof coaches produced to accompany 'Lord of the Isles' in 1961 were eventually replaced with new scale clerestory coaches in 1982.

Toys, Kool Kats, Yawnies, Karate Kid and Flower Fairies. The new MD began to reverse the emphasis of Hornby Railways from greater realism and scale accuracy towards a more toy-like approach by introducing a number of brightly coloured 0-4-0 tank locomotives for younger children while cutting back on the development of scale models at the top of the range.

The result was that after the introduction of an amazing seven new locomotives in 1981, only four were introduced in the next five years. One of these was an adaptation of an earlier model, which is a very different thing from being a new version of an existing model: new versions were created by producing existing locomotive types with new names, numbers or liveries; the adaptation

involved modifying the tools themselves, and effectively provided Hornby with a new class of locomotive for very little extra cost. This was the Great Western Saint Class 4-6-0 (first introduced in 1986), which was made by adapting the tools that had been used to produce the Tri-ang Hornby Hall class model discussed in Chapter Three. The entirely new locomotives that appeared during this period were the Class 110 DMU (diesel multiple unit) and the Class 58 Diesel in 1982, and a scale model of the Princess Royal class in 1984.

As with the electrical multiple unit (EMU), diesel multiple units, which were introduced to the national rail network during the 1950s, provided BR with many logistical advantages, because they

were 'self-propelled' and did not need a separate locomotive. Hornby's model was of the Class 110 DMU (popularly known as the 'Calder Valley' class), which was built by the Birmingham Railway Carriage & Wagon Co for BR in order to provide suburban and cross-country passenger services, especially in Lancashire and Yorkshire. Many of BR's DMUs were refurbished during the 1970s to extend their life into the 1990s, the last one being withdrawn in 1992. The Class 110 has survived a little later on Hornby Railways than on British Railways, with the most recent version released in 1999. Hornby's model is particularly attractive, with flush glazed windows, some of which are open, and full interior detail. The model has appeared with various running numbers and in four different BR liveries, and from the start was sold with a sheet of destination labels giving the choice of Bradford, Doncaster and Blackpool (early versions had a sheet of destination codes as well as the names).

The Class 58 Diesel also joined the Hornby range in 1982, a year before the real thing went into service with British Rail. In this instance Hornby had not had to be particularly quick off the mark to beat BR to it: BR's first order had been placed in 1979 but construction (by BREL at Doncaster) had been extremely slow. BR's requirements for its new freight locomotive were that it should be cheap to build, cheap to maintain, and have the potential for export (a potential which was never fulfilled). Fifty were built between 1983 and 1987 and went into service hauling coal from loading depots to power stations, many of the class being named after the power stations and depots they served.

The Hornby model was very good except for a slight discrepancy in the size of the wheels, which occurred despite the fact that the bogie was specially made for this model. The first version of the Hornby model was No 58007, released in the new grey and red Railfreight livery but with several minor errors due to the fact that Hornby's model was in the shops before the real thing was in service on the railways. These errors included having the number on all four cab sides (later versions correctly had it on the right-hand side only at each end), no 'Railfreight' insignia, a white line along the footplate and a black buffer beam (later corrected to red). Later versions included No 58001, the first of the class, and, from 1996 onwards, several models in the liveries of two other freight companies: blue for Mainline and maroon for EWS.

Mainline was one of a number of semi-independent rail freight operating companies set up by BR as a first step towards privatisation, the others being LoadHaul, Transrail, Freightliner and RES. When the various companies were offered for sale, an American company bought Mainline, LoadHaul and Transrail, and merged them to form a country-wide freight service called English, Scottish & Welsh: EW&S or EWS. One version of the Hornby Class 58 appeared with the ampersand and two without, recalling the ampersand difficulties experienced with the introduction of post-Grouping liveries to the Gauge 0 Hornby Series.

The next Hornby locomotive to be introduced was a new model of the Princess Royal ('Princess') class in 1984, a more accurate, scale model of the toy 'Princess' with which the

Rovex story had begun. Unfortunately, even this 'scale' model was marred by inaccuracies in the tender and the chassis, including the fact that the driving wheels of the model were evenly spaced when they should not have been, and, most noticeably, that there was far too large a gap between the rear driving wheels and the pony truck wheels (a pony is a bogie with only one axle). The slide bars and valve gear for the model were from the Hornby Class 4P 2-6-4 Tank, which looked correct on most of the 'Princesses' but should not have been used for models of the first two members of the class, No 6200 'The Princess Royal' and No 6201 'Princess Elizabeth'. As well as being the first two members of the class, these were also the first two 'Princesses' to be produced by Hornby, in 1984 and 1986 respectively, both in LMS maroon livery. Hornby's model of 'The Princess Royal' was released with the Fowler-style tender used for Hornby's Deeley Compound, which was too small for a correctly scaled model, and all subsequent models of the 'Princess' class were released with a larger Stanier-type tender. The Princess Royal after whom the LMS locomotive was named was Princess Mary of Harewood, the only daughter of George V.

Above The 1977 range Mk 3 coaches was replaced in 1999 by scale-length Mk 3s, seen here in four different liveries.

In the same year that 'The Princess Royal' was introduced to the mainstream Hornby range, a hugely popular group of locomotives joined the 'play' range: Thomas the Tank Engine and Friends. Push-along models of Thomas, Gordon, James and Percy were introduced in 1984, with electric versions of Thomas and Percy following in 1985, an electric Gordon in 1986, and electric versions of many other characters having been introduced since. Thomas the Tank Engine was the creation of the Reverend Wilbert Awdrey, of whom the London *Evening Standard* said that: 'The name of the Rev W Awdrey probably means little to most people but mention Gordon, Henry or the Fat Controller to anyone brought up since the last war and the recognition should be instantaneous.'

The Rev Awdrey's books were inspired by stories he had told to his young son and by his own model railway. The original Thomas on Awdrey's model railway was an 0-6-0 Tank made by pre-war manufacturer Stewart Reidpath, but he replaced this in 1978 with a Tri-ang Hornby Jinty which he painted blue. He later replaced the Jinty with a repainted Hornby E2 Tank Locomotive, and it was this model which, appropriately, was to be the starting point for Hornby's version of Thomas, although the Hornby models were based not on the illustrations in Awdrey's books but on the subsequent television series.

The Hornby E2 Tank Locomotive was withdrawn in 1985, having appeared in just three variations, and the body tool was then altered to create Thomas. The first pre-production sample was rejected because the face did not look right and because the locomotive body still looked too much like the E2, retaining the same cab, bunker and short chimney. A second sample was made which was approved and then successfully went into production – both pre-production samples have survived in private collections. The most recent addition to the Hornby range of Thomas the Tank Engine and Friends was Henry the

Above The new face of the E2 – the Rev Awdrey's own 'Thomas' was a repainted Hornby Class E2 tank, and in 1985 Hornby followed his lead by altering the existing tooling of the E2 to produce the ever-popular 'Thomas the Tank Engine'.

Green Engine in 2002, at a time when the company was being pressed for more models in the Thomas series. The Black Five had just been retooled as a super-detailed model, making the old tooling redundant, and so the original Black Five changed its colours and became Henry.

1984 was a year for glamour, because as well as Princesses and television stars, the subject of an Andy Warhol painting – the Campbell's soup can – was also modelled by Hornby. Campbell's was the company livery used on the first of a series of curtain-sided wagons introduced to the range in 1984, having first been used on the national network in 1981. This type of van came into being after there had been some problems with the doors of the existing vans being jammed by pallets of canned soup that had shifted during transportation. As a result, eight pallet vans from a fleet operated by BRTE for Campbell's Soups Ltd had their wooden sides and doors removed and curtain sides fitted instead, and a batch of 20 slightly longer curtain-siders was built by Procor in 1982. (BRTE was the British Railway Traffic & Electric Co, which was established in 1902 as a rolling stock hire company and was acquired by

Procor in 1974.) The curtains of both types were of woven polyester sheet coated with PVC and lacquer and were fastened to nylon runners with straps along the bottom of each side to tension the curtain. The Hornby model appears to be based on the original eight vans, although it has also appeared in liveries applicable to later versions.

There was no new locomotive in 1985, but there were additions to Hornby's passenger rolling stock with the introduction of a rack of new BR Mk 3 coaches. These had eight windows on each side and replaced the existing Mk 3 stock which had been produced, incorrectly, with only seven windows. Two variations of the new Mk 3 stock were produced, one set with buffers for locomotive-hauled trains and one without for use with the High-Speed Train. The following year saw another interesting addition to the range of goods wagons, with the introduction of the Harvey Bros Livestock Wagon. This wagon was manufactured using a body moulding that had first been used at least 30 years earlier, making it the longest surviving body moulding to have been designed by Rovex; models continued to be made using this moulding until 1994 and the wagon

HORNBY® 00 SCALE MODEL RAILWAYS · FORTY-THIRD EDITION 1997

LOCOMOTIVES
TOP LINK
FROM HORNBY

L N E R

4472

The legend is alive

Left This 1997 catalogue cover nods to the Hornby tradition while looking to the future.

Above Curtain-sided vans were not very successful on the real railways, unlike with the Hornby range where, from 1984, they ran to at least seven different liveries.

Below By the mid-1990s, the oldest surviving model was the cattle wagon, which had first been marketed by Tri-ang in 1956. This final version of the model was last seen in the catalogue in 1996 – exactly 40 years later!

was still in the catalogue two years later, a lifespan of fully 40 years before it was finally withdrawn. It is uncertain exactly when the first cattle wagon to use this moulding became available but it was either Christmas or spring 1956: the model was certainly advertised in the February 1956 *Railway Modeller*. Unlike most of the early wagons it underwent few changes in the 1950s and 1960s, but it came into its own in the 1980s and 1990s when it was released in the liveries of the SR, LMS and GWR as well as the private ownership livery of Harvey Bros in 1986.

On 10 December 1986 Hornby's parent company, Wiltminster Ltd, was floated on the Unlisted Securities Market as Hornby Group plc. This meant that the Hornby name now occupied all three tiers of the company hierarchy: the Hornby Railways brand was manufactured by Hornby Hobbies Ltd, which was owned by the

new Hornby Group plc. To celebrate the flotation, 34 red-bodied versions of Hornby's 0-4-0 Pug Saddle Tank Locomotive were produced, printed in gold with 'Hornby USM Debut December 1986'. (The Class 0F 'Caledonian Pug', of which this was a variation, had been introduced to the Hornby range in 1980.) Reporting on the flotation in the *Daily Telegraph* of 31 January 1987, Maurice Weaver wrote:

There is a place in England where the trains still roll off the production line in the livery of the LNER and LMS, where the locos have chimneys, signal arms fall with a satisfying clunk and engineers talk of 4-6-2 configurations, pannier tanks and push-rods.

All in double-0 gauge, of course. The Hornby company, the very stuff of a million boyhood memories, is getting up steam after December's City flotation and doing very comfortably, thank you, down at Margate in Kent.

The influx of working capital resulting from the flotation allowed the company to expand, and the success of the Scalextric and Hornby Railways brands in particular led to investment in those two areas, with the number of new locomotives being once again briefly on the increase. There were five new introductions in the next two years: the Class 142 'Pacer' DMU and the Class 06 Diesel Shunter in 1987, and the 8F, the Class 90 Electric and Class 91 Electric in 1988, a year which also saw the introduction of new Mk 4 coaches.

British Rail's Class 142 'Pacer' was a two-axle diesel railcar built as a significant improvement on the Class 141 which had been introduced in 1984 and had suffered from numerous mechanical problems while in service. Many of these resulted from poor power pick-up, a problem more often associated with model trains than the real thing. The 'Pacers' were a development of the railbus concept and consisted of twin units seating 96 passengers. The individual units were more akin to buses than trains and have been described as being 'virtually a Leyland single-decker bus mounted on railway frames and wheels'[i]. DMUs were given a running number ('set number') as well as each unit having its own individual car number. The Hornby model first appeared in the light and dark blue livery of BR's Provincial Sector, with the cars numbered 55589 and 55639 and a choice of set numbers, the set number illustrated

Uniquely among locomotives, examples of the 8F had been built by all four of the big railway companies, which had been co-opted to do so by the Ministry of Supply before and during World War II. More than 800 8Fs were built and saw service on all regions of BR, making it a very good locomotive to model despite the fact that Wrenn was still producing the former Hornby-Dublo model.

The new Hornby Railways 8F had a glowing firebox and a fully detailed cab with glazed windows. In most model locomotives the distance between the locomotive and the tender has to be artificially large (i.e. not to scale) in order for the

in the catalogue being 142048. Hornby's 'Pacer' was later released in various BR regional liveries and later in the blue livery of the private operator Northern Spirit.

The 8F appeared in the Hornby Railways catalogue in 1988, 30 years after a die-cast-body version had been produced by Meccano in the Hornby-Dublo range. (In fact the new Hornby model did not become available until 1989, despite appearing in the 1988 catalogue.)

model to make it round the tight curves of a model layout (again, tighter than a strictly scaled version would allow), but in the case of the model 8F the correct close coupling was achieved by an ingenious springing device between locomotive and tender. The tender itself was quite important because a new 15-foot wheelbase tender drive unit was made for this model and was later used for other models including the 'Princess' and the Black Five. The only slight disadvantage of the 8F

Left Once again keeping pace with modern railway development, Hornby released its model of the single pantograph Class 90 electric in 1988. Many versions of the Class 90 were made during the 1990s including four in the livery of Virgin Trains – pictured is 'British Transport Police', which was released in 1998.

Above A modern diesel multiple unit arrived in 1987 in the form of the two-car Pacer, which was fast becoming a familiar sight on branch lines in Britain. The Pacer appeared in various BR liveries as well as that of the private company Northern Spirit, seen here.

Below Paradise Found in the Far East? The Class 92 electric locomotive was the first Hornby model to be tooled in China – seen here is No 92020 'Milton'.

as a subject to model was that it only ever appeared in two liveries, which were both the same colour – LMS black and BR black. Nonetheless, Hornby managed to produce 11 different versions and even managed a special limited edition in grey.

This prolific period of locomotive production for Hornby was followed by a protracted period of consolidation. Five new locomotives had been introduced in 1987 and 1988, but only two were introduced in the next seven years: the Class 2800 and the Class D 0-4-0T, both in 1991. As well as new models, the post-flotation cash influx had been spent on modernising the production

process with automation and computer-control. Nearly £1 million was spent in 1988 on new tooling, machinery and equipment and on strengthening quality control; the following year this expenditure was almost doubled, while the turnover and profits of the Hornby Group also increased. However, boom soon came perilously close to bust. In 1991 turnover dropped for the first time in a decade and, mainly as a result of the collapse of a French subsidiary, profits for the Hornby Group fell by more than half. It had not exactly been a rollercoaster ride, but what had seemed like a steady climb of reduced losses and

then increasing profits since the management buyout in 1981 was suddenly in danger of turning into a sickening plunge in the other direction.

In the mid-1990s the number of management staff was reduced by 15, and the managing director, Keith Ness, left the company. Once again Hornby Railways was forced to regroup and once again it came out fighting, with two completely new models of locomotives having a European flavour (the Class 92 Electric was introduced in 1995 and the Class 373 Eurostar in 1996), and *22* updated models based on existing tooling also released in 1996. These included the re-release of the Class B12 4-6-0, which had first been introduced by Tri-ang Railways in 1963 and had not been produced since 1979.

The Class 92 Electric marked several firsts, both on the real railways and for Hornby. The model was the first Hornby locomotive to be made in China and the first to be released in the new Top Link packaging that was introduced in 1995. The initial version of the model represented No 92009 'Elgar', which was the first of the real Class 92s to be built. The class was built for Railfreight Distribution and SNCF for use at either end of the Channel Tunnel. (SNCF is the Société Nationale des Chemins de Fer, or National Society of Iron Roads, the French national railway company.) All versions of the Hornby model represented British-liveried members of the class, all with the correct Tunnel insignia and all named after British luminaries: No 92020 'Milton', No 92022 'Charles Dickens', No 92026 'Britten' and No 92045 'Chaucer'. Just as there had been a race between Trix and Tri-ang

Hornby to produce the 'Flying Scotsman' in 1968, so the race was now on between Hornby Hobbies and rival manufacturer Lima to produce the Class 92. Both models appeared in 1995, the Hornby model looking superior to the Lima version. The only disappointment was that the overhead pantograph was a dummy and not wired for current collection as it had been on the E3000/Class 81 in 1966.

The Channel Tunnel was officially opened in May 1994, an event which saw the realisation of a project first envisioned nearly 200 years earlier. The first detailed

Left In the same year as the Class 90 came the Class 91, looking somewhat truncated here without its train in tow. Many named locomotives were released during the next 14 years including, in 1994, 'The Scotsman' – named after the newspaper, not after a male inhabitant of the nation.

proposals had been put forward after the Treaty of Amiens in 1802, a brief and uneasy peace in the Napoleonic Wars between Britain and France. The plans were for two tunnels that would be used by horse-drawn coaches and would meet at an artificial island mid-Channel, with stabling facilities for the horses. This plan was never put into action because war broke out again within a year of the Treaty, and Napoleon began planning an invasion of England. The arrival of the railways made the idea of a tunnel far more realistic, and two railway companies actually began digging tunnels towards the end of the 19th century, but both schemes were abandoned in 1883. The idea was then approved and shelved several times by parliament until 1981, when Prime Minister Margaret Thatcher and President Mittérand put their signatures to the Treaty of Canterbury and at last the Channel Tunnel was begun.

Work began in 1987 and the breakthrough of the marine service tunnel was made in December 1990, joining Britain and mainland Europe for the first time (and, in a sense, robbing Britain of its island status). The Channel Tunnel is in fact three tunnels: two parallel rail tunnels with a smaller service tunnel running between them which provides a continuous safe haven if passengers have to be evacuated from a train. For the inauguration ceremony the Queen first opened Waterloo International Station in London

Above Echoes of Hornby-Dublo – a very attractive model of the LMS Class 8F had been introduced to the Dublo range in 1958, and exactly 30 years later a brand-new 8F was designed and released by Hornby Railways.

before travelling on the Eurostar passenger train to meet President Mittérand in Calais and then returning with him in the Queen's Rolls Royce on 'Le Shuttle'.

As well as the Class 92, the Tunnel provided another addition to the Hornby range, although this was less successful: the Class 373 Eurostar. The reason for poor sales may have been that the Eurostar was seen as having such a specific function that it could not easily be integrated into a general layout, but the model also proved to be a poor performer. The first Eurostar to be marketed by Hornby was an H0 scale model produced for the French company Jouef in Slovenia and

packaged by Hornby in 1995 both as a train pack and as a set (i.e. with or without track). Jouef went bust and, in the short term, Hornby was forced to buy its supplies from Slovenia. By 1996 all this had changed: Hornby had tooled-up its own 00 Gauge version and in the meantime Jouef was bought by the Lima Group, which decided to replace its own planned model of the Eurostar with an improved version of the Jouef model. Once again, the race was on between Hornby and Lima and once again both models were produced at the same time.

The Hornby model, which consisted of two driving units and two standard class coaches, was described as 'a little overgeared', with a tendency to fly off the tracks if run at full throttle: much the same could be said of the real thing, which needs to travel at considerably slower speeds on the English side of the tunnel, although the track is currently being upgraded. Several versions of the Hornby model subsequently appeared in Eurotunnel grey livery as well as one in GNER blue: GNER (Great North Eastern Railway) uses a Class 373 for its 'White Rose' service from York to London King's Cross.

1995 had been a significant year for the development of Hornby Railways because it had seen the introduction of the first locomotives to be made in China. 1996 brought another far-reaching change, with the acquisition of tools from erstwhile competitors Dapol, including many from the now-defunct Airfix system. By the mid-1990s competition in model railways had become a merry-go-round, just as it had in commerce and industry, with companies buying up competitors and then continuing to produce what had been competing brands under the auspices of the new company. By now the public was inured to these changes and, after all the furore there had been over the transfer of the Hornby name to Tri-ang products in 1965, 32 years later no-one batted an eyelid when Hornby began to produce models using the former Airfix and Dapol tools.

Dapol was named after its founders, *Da*vid and *Pol*ly (Pauline) Boyle, who had set up the company to market former Airfix products and spares after Airfix had gone into liquidation. Dapol subsequently produced models using tools formerly belonging to Airfix, Kitmaster, Palitoy (Mainline), British Trix/Lilliput, G & R Wrenn and Tri-ang Model-Land. At one time Dapol had an exhibition at the company's factory in Llangollen that included some machines and tools, acquired from Wrenn, that had started life in the Hornby-Dublo production line at the Meccano factory in Liverpool. Following a disastrous fire at Dapol's Winsford factory in Cheshire during 1996, Hornby bought many of Dapol's tools, including most of those for the former Airfix models and those for some excellent models originated by Dapol itself. The purchase did not include any of the former Hornby-Dublo tools.

Hornby immediately began to improve the tools and put them into production, and the first of the models to be manufactured using the new tools were introduced in 1997. The acquisition of the new tools enabled Hornby to make a huge expansion of the range in a very short time, to the tune of 13 new locomotives in three years. These were: the Class 14XX, Castle and Hawksworth County, all in 1997; the L&Y Pug, Class A1X Terrier, Class J94 Austerity, Class 4F,

Class 56 Co-Co Diesel and Class 2361 Dean Goods in 1998; and the Class 2P, Class 155 'Super Sprinter' and Class 61XX Prairie Tank in 1999, which all used tools acquired from Dapol and which were all manufactured at the Sanda Kan factory in China. In addition the 'Networker' DMU (1997) was manufactured using tools designed by Hornby.

Above Home, sweet home – new building kits introduced in 1990 included one representing the Hornby factory at Margate.

Below In 1996 the Hornby Railways Eurostar added un peu de joie de vivre to many a Christmas stocking.

This comprehensive expansion of the range was just the boost Hornby needed after the upheavals of 1995, and from 1997 onwards Hornby has been on the up – although there is a certain irony in the fact that the Dapol tools were offered to competitors Bachmann before they were offered to Hornby, so these very models could have

The ex-Dapol Castle (another GWR Collett locomotive) provided Hornby with further echoes of Hornby-Dublo and Gauge 0, both of which had included Castles in their range. The Dapol model was itself an improvement on the Airfix Castle, and the first version of the modern Hornby model was No 5042 'Winchester Castle', which came

been competing against Hornby rather than being the vanguard of the company's recovery. 1997 signalled a change in Hornby's fortunes, coinciding with yet another change of name – Hornby Railways became simply 'Hornby'.

The first of the new wave of models was the Class 14XX 0-4-2 Tank Locomotive, which was manufactured using ex-Airfix tools that were already at the Sanda Kan factory in China. The 14XX on which the model was based was a GWR tank locomotive designed by Charles Collett for light branch-line operation and introduced in 1932, initially designated the Class 48XX. Ninety-five were built, and all were withdrawn between 1954 and 1964, four of them being preserved. The first Hornby version of the model appeared in August 1997, and retained the fine detailing for which it had been famous when produced by Airfix but with the added bonus of a great improvement in performance.

as part of a train pack with three crimson and cream ex-Airfix Centenary coaches. Hornby later released the model under the names and numbers of several other members of the class, all of them in BR green livery.

The Hawksworth County 4-6-0 was yet another GWR locomotive, designed by F W Hawksworth and introduced in 1945, by which time all of the earlier Churchward County 4-4-0s (represented in Hornby Gauge 0 and the Hornby Railways range) had been withdrawn. Thirty Hawksworth Counties were built in two years between 1945 and 1947 and were essentially powerful two-cylinders version of the Castle. The Hornby version first appeared in 1997 as No 1004 'County of Somerset' in GWR green livery, part of a train pack that included three GWR Centenary coaches. Later versions included other members of the class in GWR green, BR green and BR black.

Above The five faces of 'Sir Ralph Wedgewood'. In 1939, A4 class locomotive No 4469 'Gadwall' in LNER garter blue was renamed 'Sir Ralph Wedgewood' after one of the directors of the LNER, but in 1942 this locomotive was destroyed in York station by a German bomb. As a replacement, No 4466 'Herring Gull', by now in wartime black, was renamed 'Sir Ralph Wedgewood'. No 4466 survived the rest of the war and carried the name 'Sir Ralph Wedgewood' into BR green livery with the new number 60006, to be finally decommissioned in 1965. Hornby recorded this unusual story with the five models shown here – the three versions of 'Sir Ralph Wedgewood' were all produced in 1994 (and were available in a boxed set), while 'Gadwall' and 'Herring Gull' appeared the following year.

Above As well as buying the tools for locomotives from Dapol in 1996, Hornby also bought those for a number of wagons and coaches. The most attractive wagon was the Vee Tanker, which has been produced in a number of liveries including that of Ketton Cement, seen here.

Below When is a castle not a castle? When it's a palace. This GWR Castle class locomotive is named after Blenheim Palace, the home of the Dukes of Wellington and the only palace in the country that is not either royal or episcopal. First released in 1997, later versions of this ex-Dapol model had a new, Hornby-designed stepped tender.

The three ex-Dapol models which were released in 1997 were followed by another six in 1998. The first of these was a model of the L&Y Pug, an 0-4-0 saddle tank locomotive that originated on the Lancashire and Yorkshire Railway in 1891. The 'Pug' was designed by Sir John Audley Frederick Aspinall, who later became Associate Professor of Railway Engineering at Liverpool University, and whose locomotives have been described as 'simple and robust'[ii]. The Pug was used for dock shunting duties, its short wheelbase allowing it to manage tight curves. It continued to be used by the LMS and later BR, in both of whose black liveries it was produced by Hornby. The model was beautiful and finely detailed, the only criticism being that the motor was obtrusively visible in the cab, a problem arising from the diminutive size of the original locomotive, which was even smaller than the Caledonian Pug which had already been modelled by Hornby.

Hornby's ex-Dapol model of the Class A1X 'Terrier' 0-6-0 Tank Locomotive was released at almost the same time as the Pug, first appearing in Southern green livery and later in BR black and LBSC Marsh umber. As with the Pug, this tank locomotive had its origins in the 19th century, having been introduced to the LBSC in 1872, more than 125 years before the Hornby model was released. The Terrier, so-called because of its remarkable acceleration, was designed by William Stroudley and had a distinctive tall, narrow chimney, and was used for shunting and light passenger duties. One of the class was awarded a Gold Medal at the Paris Exhibition of 1878 and two others (Nos 32636 and 32670, both produced by Hornby in 2000) were the oldest locomotives in service on British Railways during the 1960s. Several are still in operation on Britain's preserved steam railways, including 'Fenchurch', which can be seen on the Bluebell Railway and is the oldest standard gauge locomotive still in steam in the UK. Hornby's model was well received by the model railway press, *Model Railway Enthusiast* saying that:

The long awaited Hornby Terrier Tank (R2063) has arrived and what a beautiful model it is. It comes complete with even the vacuum pipes in place. Despite this there is a bag of bits in the box which allows you, with suitable skills, to change the model to reflect alterations to the prototype. The bag contains a steam dome and safety valves, a different coal bunker, two extra pieces of pipework and a ring with which to extend the boiler. This does not mean that the model is plugged together like a toy kit and all you have to do is pull it to pieces and reassemble it with different parts. The finish of the model would not look as good as it does if it had been constructed to allow that level of flexibility. The spare parts are for people who know what they are doing. Hornby do not provide a hack saw but you will need one.

This is a very attractive model, finely printed, and one that many will be proud to add to their stud.

The Pug and the Terrier were joined in the same year by yet another tank locomotive, the famous Class J94 'Austerity' 0-6-0 Saddle Tank. The model was based on a locomotive designed by Robert Riddles for the Ministry of Supply during World War II, itself based on a Hunslet industrial locomotive which was at the time being supplied to steel works. Examples of the Riddles version (with larger wheels) were built between 1944 and 1947 to perform heavy shunting duties for the war effort on both sides of the Channel. Nearly 100 more were later built for industrial firms, mainly the National Coal Board, bringing the total to 484 by the time the last one was built in 1964; some 50 of those 484 have been preserved. Immediately after the war 75 Austerities were transferred to the LNER where they were designated Class J94, and it was in LNER black livery that the Hornby model first appeared. Later versions included BR black, LMR blue, NCB red and NCB green. The model appeared in British shops in July 1998 and, like the real 'Austerity', it proved to be a very powerful model, despite its small size. It also went down well on the aesthetic front: the *Model Railway Enthusiast* reviewer showed his enthusiasm by commenting that: 'The body detailing is very good indeed and a nice touch is the sprung buffers. An excellent model!'

As well as 19th-century and World War II tank locomotives, in 1998 the Class 56 Co-Co Diesel was first manufactured, using tools that had originated with Mainline (Palitoy) and had come to Hornby via Dapol. The Class 56 was introduced to BR in 1976 to haul coal trains, and 60 of the type were eventually built, which at the time were the most powerful diesel locomotives in service in Britain. As with the 'Austerity', the model Class 56 proved to be extremely powerful, impressing the *Model Railway Enthusiast* with its capabilities:

Wow! What a Load it Hauled!

[The headline was a pun on LoadHaul, whose livery the locomotive carried.]

The normal maximum load limit for a Class 56 diesel locomotive is 36 wagons. The new Hornby model pulled 43 with the greatest of ease before we ran out of space on the MRE test track. In fact, the locomotive had joined up with the train's tail!

Above
Top The former London Brighton & South Coast Railway 'Terrier' tank has long been a firm favourite. The 'Terrier' is seen here in LBSC livery as 'Waddon' (released in 2000 as a limited edition of 1000 models).
Bottom The Class 14XX 0-4-2 GWR tank, released in 1997, was the first model to be produced using tools acquired from Dapol in 1996. Hornby carried out modifications to improve the performance of the model before putting it into production.

Above The BR 4-6-2 'Clan Line' Merchant Navy Class is so detailed it could almost be mistaken for the full-scale train itself.

. . . The models are nicely detailed, as were the Dapol originals with their driver and guard in the cab and the cab end detail. Hornby, however, have added their own improvements including wire cab side handrails, blackened wheels, an improved shade of yellow on the cabs and phosphor-bronze current pick-up wipers on all six wheels on the trailing bogie.

The Class 56 model initially appeared in four versions: as No 56100 in the black and orange livery of the LoadHaul freight company with a limited edition of 500 as No 56118 in the same livery; and as No 56058 in the maroon of EW&S, again with a limited edition of 500, in this case as No 56105. Hornby also cleverly released ex-Dapol models of an HEA hopper wagon in both liveries at the same time as the locomotives. (HEA describes a *H*opper type *E* with *A*ir brakes.) The model later appeared in the grey livery of BR Transrail, the grey and yellow 'Dutch' livery of Transrail and, in 2002, in BR blue and in the red and gold of EWS (by then the ampersand had been dropped).

Hornby's production of new models continued in 1999 with the ex-Mainline Class 2P 4-4-0. This was a correctly scaled version of the locomotive modelled by Hornby Railways in 1973, which was itself a modification of the Tri-ang Railways Class L1 dating from 1960. (The L1 had also appeared as the Hornby Series No 2 Special for the Southern Railway in Gauge 0.) Two versions of the 2P were introduced to Britain's railways, the first designed by Deeley in 1912 for the Midland Railway (as rebuilds of an earlier class of locomotive built by Samuel Johnson from 1882 to 1901), and the second developed from Deeley's 2P by Sir Henry Fowler for the LMS and introduced in 1928. The mixed heritage of the model was even more complex than that of the real thing, having been designed by Palitoy and produced as part of the Mainline range in 1984 with an Airfix tender, then acquired

by Dapol which produced several of its own versions from 1986 to 1996, and finally bought by Hornby, which by the end of 2000 had produced six versions in LMS and BR black liveries and two in the blue of the Somerset & Dorset Joint Railway. The influence of Airfix could be seen in the fact that this was the only Palitoy-designed model to have the motor in the tender, the tender having been designed by Airfix rather than in-house by Palitoy.

The other new model steam locomotive to be released in 1999 had a similarly complicated past. It was the Class 61XX 2-6-2 Prairie Tank and, as *Model Railway Enthusiast* pointed out, 'It has been a long road from the Airfix GWR Prairie launched in 1977 to the Hornby model released 22 years later in 1999.' Airfix produced two versions of the model from 1977 to 1981, Mainline two versions from 1983 to 1984, Dapol four versions from 1985 to 1994, and Hornby released two versions in 1999 with four more in the next three years, all but two in Great Western green livery. However, the model had changed along the way and *MRE* approved of the changes: 'The model released in October appears to be a far cry from the original Airfix version not least because of the improvements to it made

Left The Lancashire & Yorkshire 'Pug' 0-4-0 saddle tank is the smallest locomotive in the current Hornby range. The main criticism of this otherwise beautifully detailed model was the fact that the motor was obtrusively visible in the cab, as can be seen all too clearly in this photograph.

Below Another beautifully recreated model of a beautifully designed original was the 'Austerity' 0-6-0 saddle tank, released by Hornby in 1998. The 'Austerity' had widespread industrial use after the World War II, so many liveries are available, providing a very colourful stable.

Right Looking particularly authentic in this superbly weathered version, the Class 56 is the best diesel model in the Hornby catalogue. It was introduced in 1998, with this factory-weathered model released in 2002.

Below The Hawksworth County class, looking very different from the Churchward County represented by both Gauge 0 and Hornby Railways.

by Hornby themselves. These include chassis, motor, wheels, smokebox door, filler vents, lamp brackets and separate handrails.'The first Hornby versions were No 6113 and a limited edition of 1000 as No 6150.

As well as these steam locomotives with roots dating back almost a century, Hornby also released another DMU in 1999, the ex-Dapol Class 155 Super Sprinter. The class on which the model was based had been designed and built by the Leyland Bus Company and entered service in the late 1980s as a replacement in some areas for the Class 150, which in turn had entered service in 1985, operating in twin- or three-car sets. The Class 155 was the first BR DMU to have longer, 23-metre cars each carrying 80 passengers. The model first appeared in the maroon and cream livery of the West Yorkshire Metro and the following year in the grey and blue of the Provincial. Although the Dapol model had been refined by Hornby, it still did not perform

particularly well because of problems with the motor bogie.

As well as the introduction of these new models, 1999 also saw one particularly interesting variation of an existing model: a limited edition of 500 examples of the 2-10-0 9F as No 92203 'Black Prince'. 'Evening Star' was famously the only 9F to be named by BR (the name was chosen in recognition of the fact that it was the last steam locomotive to be built), and artist David Shepherd caused quite a stir among the purists when he rescued No 92203 from scrapping and named it 'Black Prince': 'I named her "Black Prince" just after I bought her. People said, "What do you want to give it a name for, it never had a name." She's now known as "Black Prince" because she's carried the name for four times her working life. She was only eight years old on BR, and I've owned her since 1967. Of course she's "Black Prince". She *knows* she's "Black Prince".'

David Shepherd nearly upset the purists once again when he decided to alter the livery of 'Black Prince' by lining it out, but he subsequently reverted to the original: 'I decided in a very unwise moment to line

her out in red. I rang up this signwriter and I said, "I've got an engine, I'd love it if you could line her out for me." I was driving him to the site and by halfway there he'd established that it wasn't double-0. He said, "Well what gauge is it?" and then we turned round the corner and he saw Black Prince, all 140 tons of her. Anyway, he lined her out but it didn't look right so I painted it out again.'

The 'Black Prince' version of Hornby's 9F model reverted to the BR1 type tender, and benefitted from a revised chassis which had been perfected in China earlier that year. The release of this model had been predicted a year earlier by *Model Railway Enthusiast*, which reported having seen Simon Kohler, Hornby's Marketing Manager, engaged in 'lengthy discussions with the owner' at the 1998 Warley National Model Railway Exhibition. David Shepherd confirms this, describing how the model came to be:

I met Simon Kohler at the Warley Model Railway Exhibition, at this crazy mad thing, it could only happen in England. The Warley Model Railway Club hire a hall at the NEC – you could land a 747 in there. They asked if they could have 'Black Prince' as the star attraction and I thought they must be joking. Anyway, to cut a long story short, the transport people inspected the site and they said it was no problem – 'Black Prince' to them is a small load. So in she came on the low loader, two in the morning into this massive hall, we'd already laid the track on the floor. The exhibition opened at 10 o'clock with 'Black Prince' on her track and then she went out again on Sunday evening, it was just incredible. That's where I met Simon Kohler, and he said that Hornby would give £10,000 towards the cost of her overhaul. The money came by selling the limited edition of 'Black Prince'. It was a gift from heaven, it really was – well, it was a gift from Hornby.

It was his father who introduced David Shepherd to steam and model railways, but despite founding a preserved railway and owning two steam locomotives he says that he knows nothing about the technicalities of railways. He just loves trains:

When my sister and my brother and I went down to Kent in the 1930s for the summer holidays Daddy said 'We don't want to build sandcastles on the beach, let's go and watch the trains go by.' So that's what we did, and that's the bug. When my father had a model railway [a Hornby Gauge 0] we lived in Totteridge in north London and he took over

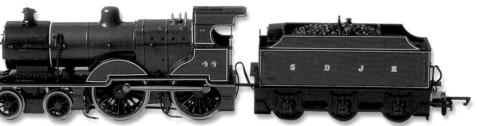

the best bedroom in the house, which model railway enthusiasts do sometimes, and he bored a hole right through the chimney breast to make a tunnel so that you could get a better curve from Euston by the door to Crewe in the window. If the chimney smokes in that house now, that's why!

I know nothing about the technicalities of an engine. I haven't a clue what goes on inside 'Black Prince', it's what she does when you light her up. She. She's a member of my family. I love 'Black Prince'. If anything happened to her I'd be devastated. People say, 'How can you go patting an engine?' When she's been in steam all day, giving enormous pleasure to huge numbers of people, I go round patting her afterwards …

Below In 1999 Hornby's ex-Mainline model of the Class 2P 4-4-0, seen here, appeared as a correctly scaled version of the locomotive first produced by Hornby Railways more than a quarter of a century earlier. The new Hornby model appeared in LMS and BR liveries as well as in the smart dark blue of the Somerset & Dorset Joint Railway.

Right After extensive modifications to improve both appearance and performance, Hornby released the former Airfix GWR Prairie tank in 1999 to the great approval of the model railway press.

Below Is it a bus? Is it a train? No, it's… the Class 155 Super Sprinter, designed and built by the Leyland Bus Company. The model, originally developed by Dapol, was refined by Hornby but still did not perform well, despite the improvements.

She's like a horse, and if you don't know how to ride, the horse will immediately know and start fooling around. Steam engines are exactly the same. Just after I bought 'Black Prince' she was allowed out on a couple of excursions on British Rail's main line. She ran from Cranmore on the East Somerset Railway [a preserved railway founded by David Shepherd] up to Oxford with our own crew, who knew how to tend 'Black Prince' and loved her.

When we got to Oxford Station BR took over, with a BR crew and the thirteen coaches we were taking down to Hereford, via Worcester. This BR fireman didn't know how to fire her. I was on the footplate, and it was very funny. He thought you just shoved the coal through the hole in the firebox door. You don't, you've got to cover the whole grate. 'Black Prince' immediately knew he couldn't fire her so the boiler pressure needle dropped, dropped, dropped, *dropped, she started going slower and slower; and the slower she went the more he swore – and the more coal he shovelled in. By the time we got to Worcester we were about twenty minutes late and we had to practically carry him off the footplate. The next fireman gets on, and he sees the needle right down there, and he says, 'What's the matter with you, you old cow' and he kicks her. Well, that's a slight exaggeration but it's more or less what happened. And then 'Black Prince' knew she couldn't fool and the needle rose and we made up that twenty minutes by the time we got to Hereford.*

The following year was 2000, and Hornby celebrated the millennium in style with a special limited edition gold-plated 'Flying Scotsman', the Hornby Virtual Railway, a special individually numbered 46th edition of the catalogue, and the Rebuilt Merchant Navy.

Hornby had entered the computer age in 1980 with the Zero 1 control system, but at the turn of the 21st century the company took the computer interface a step further with HVR, the Hornby Virtual Railway. Conceived as a track planning tool, Hornby's publicity explains that it allows users to create model railway layouts in a new dimension: 'For many years a piece of graph paper, protractor and the Hornby Track Plans Book have been one of the few ways of planning a model railway layout. But not anymore. Now the R8120 Hornby Virtual Railway is here. Creating a model railway layout has never been so easy!'

Hornby worked with software experts Vega Skillchange to produce a programme which allowed users to design layouts using a database of trains, tracks and accessories, which would then provide them with an accurate shopping list so that they could buy the right components in the knowledge that the layout would work. There were six basic pieces of track to give beginners an understanding of track design, and HVR also provided the option of creating complete layouts from scratch – clicking on the 'loco' icon would reveal a selection of locomotives and rolling stock which could be placed on the newly-designed track layout. The trains could then be set in motion with one of six adjustable camera

positions recording the journey for playback later. And for users who did not want to ride on the train there were also the options of walking the rails, riding on the footplate or wandering through the world they had created. Furthermore, as the computer literate would fully expect, a facility launched in September 2001 meant that HVR could be updated directly from the Hornby website: at the launch of this facility, downloads included the 'Clan Line' and 'Duchess of Gloucester' locomotives, Pullman, LMS and LNER coaches, various goods wagons and a range of assorted sized trees.

Justin Etkin is the model railways expert at Hamleys toyshop in Regent Street, London, and he confirms that HVR is doing its job: 'It's proved extremely popular. A lot of customers have computers and they're using HVR. People come in with their print-outs of what they need. HVR acts like a catalogue: you've got the track and the accessories, and customers actually come in now and say, "I've designed this layout on HVR and I need this, this, this and this."'

And not only did HVR make planning a layout part of the fun rather than being a preliminary chore, it also introduced a new audience to model railways by appealing to 'the hi-tech, computer-literate community who in the

Right Prince of Darkness – David Shepherd upset the purists by giving his preserved 9F a name, but it is now the second most famous of its class after 'Evening Star'.

past would, without hesitation, let the fascinating world of model railways pass them by'. In other words, it was gaining back some ground from the computer games that had hit the model railway market so badly in the 1990s. This was partly because HVR, though conceived as a planning tool for physical layouts, could also be used as a virtual railway: 'Create on your PC the model railway you have always wanted, but never had the space to accommodate. Simple and easy to use, Hornby Virtual Railway allows you to bring a fully interactive working railway to your desktop . . . Once complete you can take a virtual ride through your own layout and experience each track from a passengers' eye view.'

Back in the world of physical models, expectations had been built up in 2000 by the announcement of the new 'Coronation', as they had been in 1939 by the announcement of the Hornby-Dublo Princess Coronation (delayed until after the war) and in 1970 by the Tri-ang Hornby model. This time the model first appeared as No 6229 'Duchess of Hamilton' and, once again, Hornby did not disappoint. The internet magazine *Model Railway Express* commented that: 'The model was certainly worth waiting for and makes one want to hide the 1970 Tri-ang Hornby model from sight. Gone is the small front bogie, moulded handrails on tender

and cab, the ugly raised painting lines and the much hated motor in the tender . . . We feel that anyone seeing this model will agree that Hornby are now, well and truly, on the right track.' (*Model Railway Express* is updated daily and can be found at www.mremag.demon.co.uk).

This comment is all the more significant in light of the fact that the 'Coronation' was a Hornby model through and through, showing that the company was now living up to the standards of the tooling it had bought from Dapol. Many of the ex-Dapol models had been marketed as 'Top Link' locomotives, a standard that from now on would be achieved by all the new super-detailed Hornby models.

The Rebuilt Merchant Navy class was no exception. 'Rebuilt' refers to the rebuilding of the original class of Southern Railway locomotives by British Railways, not to the model: the class was initially built with a streamlined casing and subsequently rebuilt with the casing removed and smoke deflectors fitted. Designed by Oliver Bulleid for the Southern Railway, the 4-6-2 Merchant Navy class made its first appearance in 1941 and has been described as 'a memorial to the genius of O V Bulleid'[iii], although the fairly unusual streamlined appearance of the model also resulted in members of this class being christened 'Spam Cans'. Thirty locomotives were

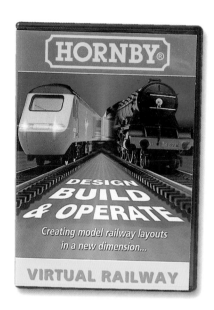

built for the SR, all of which were later rebuilt under BR from 1956 onwards. The class remained in service until 1967, when No 35030 'Elder Dempster Lines' hauled the last steam train to pull into London's Waterloo Station, in July of that year.

The first of three Hornby models to appear in 2000 was No 35028 'Clan Line' in BR green, which drew even greater praise than the Coronation. *Model Railway Express* announced :

This is an impressive product and possibly the most detailed proprietary 00 gauge railway model produced for the British market. It is certainly the finest that Hornby have produced in the 50 years their model railway system has been developing …

The plastic-centred wheels and the motion all look convincing and brass axle bearings have been fitted where needed. It has floating rear compensated drivers and application of separate detail includes boiler feed pipes, whistle with a very fine pipework and the reversing shaft which closely hugs the firebox side. The tender has finely moulded steps and ladders made in tough nylon. Metal has been used for the supporting bracket for the tender top air reservoir cowling, the tender fittings under the cab and the photo etched tender fall plate. All metal work is 'blackened' including the individually sprung buffers and all handrails are wire.

The review then went on to make some highly detailed criticisms, but concluded by saying that: 'It is easy to find faults with the very best of models as those in the trade will know. This is still the best we have seen and shows clearly that Hornby intend to take their place again amongst the world-beaters in the model railway market.' Again, evidence that while Hornby's revival may

Left The year 2000 saw the launch of the Hornby Virtual Railway. This was originally conceived as a layout planning tool but soon became a game in its own right, with update modules available from the Hornby web site, www.hornby.com

Below Stop someone on the street and ask if they can name a steam locomotive, and the chances are that they will say Stephenson's 'Rocket' or 'Flying Scotsman'. Perhaps not surprisingly, Hornby's most successful model, first introduced in 1968 and still going strong after 34 years, is Gresley's 'Flying Scotsman'. Seen here is a gold-plated model produced to commemorate the new millennium.

have been initiated by tools from elsewhere, the company was still quite capable of producing its own models to the same standard. 'Clan Line' was closely followed by two other versions released in the same year, No 35023 'Holland-Afrika Line' in BR green and No 35005 'Canadian Pacific' in BR blue. In 2002 the model was released as No 35029 'Ellerman Lines', which became the first member of Hornby's National Railway Museum Collection, a series of models representing exhibits in the NRM.

Bulleid seemed to be flavour of the new millennium, because Hornby launched a model of another Bulleid Pacific in 2001, within a year of the Merchant Navy class. This was a completely new model of the West Country class (some of which were known as the Battle of Britain class) that had previously been represented by Hornby-Dublo (in rebuilt form) and Tri-ang Railways, both of which had been introduced in 1961. The real West Country/Battle of Britain

(WC/BB) class was designed by Bulleid as a smaller version of the Merchant Navy, and was introduced to the Southern Railway in 1945, four years after its big brother. The WC/BB class locomotives were nearly two feet shorter than those of the Merchant Navy class, with driving and bogie wheels the same size as the larger locomotive but trailing wheels six inches smaller in diameter. The wheel spacing was different on the WC/BB, as correctly reproduced in the Hornby model. One hundred and ten WC/BB class locomotives were built, 60 of them later having the streamlined casings removed by BR in the same way as the Merchant Navy class. The Hornby-Dublo model had represented the 'Barnstaple' after modification, but the 2001 Hornby model represented the original version of the class with the streamlining intact, as previously modelled by Rovex in 1961.

The model first appeared as No 21C123 'Blackmoor Vale' in Southern Malachite green,

Above The 'Coronation' still looked rather bulbous even in this correctly scaled version, released in 2001 to replace the earlier foreshortened model which had been produced from 1970 until 1998.

and was unveiled on 18 September 2001 at Kingscote Signal Box on the Bluebell Railway, where the real 'Blackmoor Vale' is preserved, having been recently restored at a cost of £100,000. The model was manufactured using a special suite of tools, allowing Hornby to accurately model 85 per cent of the class. The variations possible included four types of tender, long and short smoke deflectors, and wide and narrow cabs. Three other versions of the WC/BB class appeared in the same year as 'Blackmoor Vale', all with differing body detail, and the first of these was also unveiled on 18 September, representing No 34081 '92 Squadron' in BR green livery.

'Blackmoor Vale' was modelled with short smoke deflectors and the revised wedge-shaped cab that was fitted to the real thing in 1954. The cab windows and the spectacle plates in the tender were glazed, with the cab side windows partially open. The interior of the cab was finely detailed and picked out in silver, red and copper-coloured paint, while the nameplates and coats of arms were separate additions, making them stand out correctly from the body of the locomotive. This was the third of Hornby's new super-detailed locomotives, and *Model Railway Express* was

suitably impressed, claiming that: 'It is difficult to see what more detail Hornby could add to this excellent model.'

In 2001 the new phenomenon that had caused a revival in children's literature came to Hornby – J K Rowling's Harry Potter stories. The railway connection was not quite as obvious as for *The Railway Children* or Thomas the Tank Engine, but anyone who had read the book or seen the film (and it seemed that there were few who hadn't) would have instantly recognised the Hogwarts Express. Hornby's Hogwarts Express Train Set was supplied with its own specially designed 'trakmat' (a track underlay printed with scenic details) which featured Hogwarts Castle, the lake and forest, a Quidditch arena and scenes from the film.

The locomotive was Hornby's Castle class with the name 'Hogwarts Castle' on the nameplates and the number '5972' on the cab sides. *Model Railway Express* described the model in this way:

It is in a subdued red livery, lined with BR black and orange and even has late BR decals on the new 'stepped' tender – or has it? Closer study shows that the words 'British Railways' have been replaced by 'Hogwarts Railways' and the lion and wheel by the Hogwarts coat of arms! The locomotive is also the first

Hornby Castle to come fitted with a headboard (which is plugged to the smokebox door) and this carries the name 'Hogwarts Express' and the Hogwarts coat of arms. We look forward to seeing the headboard on future releases of the model and carrying authentic train names.

The set came with two maroon BR-style coaches, Hogwarts Railways insignia, an oval of track, a siding, a transformer and a controller. It also included 'Hogsmeade' Station, made up of standard platform and fencing sections, platform accessories, a maroon coloured station halt building and 'Hogsmeade' name stickers.

The Hogwarts Express Set prompted a further upturn in Hornby's fortunes, with the company's financial performance even being reported in the national newspapers – although this may have had less to do with the sales figures than the fact that a dry financial report could be livened up by a mention and pictures of Hogwarts Express. Whether genuinely newsworthy or not, sales figures were definitely improving, partly because the Harry Potter phenomenon tapped an age group that had previously been overlooked in the model railways market. Justin Etkin of Hamleys explains the situation:

With the onset of the popularity of Playstation and other computer games, interest in model railways waned, but recently there has been a revival in the popularity of trains. Hamleys is up about 80 per cent on trains since last year. That has a lot to do with Harry Potter but also generally people are moving away from just plonking the kids in front of the computer.

It appeals to an age group that's never been that interested in trains, that eleven-, twelve-year-old age group. Before, a twelve-year-old would be more interested in a product like Scalextric, but this year we suddenly saw sales taken away from Scalextric by the Harry Potter train sets.

After the success of the scale 'Coronation' in 2000 it was a safe bet that a new 'Princess' and a new 'Duchess' would soon follow, which they duly did in 2001 and 2002 respectively. The new Princess Royal was not entirely new, the body moulding being based on the 1984 scale model, but there were numerous improvements within the body casing. The new 'Princess' appeared as No 46207 'Princess Arthur of Connaught' in LMS maroon with a new chassis and a 5-pole motor (now in the locomotive rather than the tender), as well as improvements in detail to the dome and top feed, whistle, handrails, buffers, boiler, shed plate, frame, brake hose and in the provision of cab glazing and back baffles. The 'Princess' borrowed its chassis and front bogie

Below Goodbye Margaret Rose – Hornby's 1984 model of the 'Princess' was upgraded to super-detailed status in 2001. The model pictured represents locomotive No 46203, named after Princess Margaret, who died in 2002.

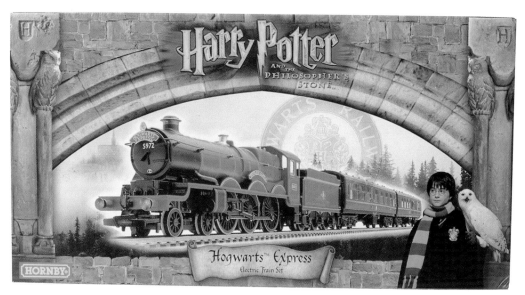

Left Harry Potter was a sell-out success in 2001... and so was the film. The Hogwarts Express train set, based on the locomotive portrayed in the film The Philosopher's Stone, sold out so quickly that a further batch of sets had to be urgently ordered from China. The set succeeded in attracting an age group that had previously been uninterested in model railways.

from the 'Coronation' but had its own specially designed motion, cylinders and pony truck.

Unlike the 'Princess', the new 'Duchess' was manufactured from completely new tooling, the fourth of the new super-detailed locomotives to be made entirely from scratch, after the Merchant Navy, the 'Coronation' and the WC/BB classes. When it finally arrived in 2002, after some delay because the cab roof profile was not right and the body moulding tool had to be revised, the 'Duchess' was available in two versions: as No 46228 'Duchess of Rutland' in BR green, and as No 6230 'Duchess of Buccleuch' in LMS maroon. *Model Railway Express* lauded the attention to detail that a decade earlier had been open to question:

Nothing has been spared to get the detail right – and what detail! ... The reproduction of the clutter on the footplate was always going to be a challenge for Hornby but it's all there and looking correct. The characteristic sand boxes, the mechanical lubricators, the feed pipe from the injector, the exhaust pipe from the ejector – they are all there. The pièce de résistance is the smokebox door which has not only a handrail and lamp brackets but the door handles are also separately attached. The detail at the rear of the tender is another high point.

Other super-detailed models announced in 2002 included an entirely new model of the Black Five (first introduced in 1973) and improved versions of the Fowler Class 4P Tank Locomotive (first introduced in 1980), the 8F (first introduced in 1988) and the King class (first introduced in 1978), all with new 5-pole motors, all-wheel pick-ups, metal handrails and other added detailing. The new Black Five was described by *Railway Modeller* as featuring 'an abundance of fine detail in the present Hornby style' and was powered by the 5-pole motor, again located in the locomotive rather than the tender. Three versions were released to mark the launch of the new model, one in black LMS livery and two in black BR, one of them weathered. *Railway Modeller* also points out that, given the locomotive's nickname, there is little

Opposite page (top) The 'Coronation' class was a streamlined version of the 'Duchess' class, so it was only logical that a brand-new model of the 'Duchess' should be tooled-up next, using the chassis already in production for the 'Coronation'. The release of the new 'Duchess' (seen here) in 2002 completed the trio of LMS Pacific models.

Right The Rebuilt Merchant Navy was quickly followed in 2001 by an un-rebuilt version of its smaller sister, the West Country/Battle of Britain class, replacing the Tri-ang model which had been produced from 1961 until 1997. A Rebuilt WC/BB class had been produced by Meccano as part of the Hornby-Dublo range from 1961–64.

scope for future livery changes, but this is not necessarily the case: the tools for Hornby's 1973 Black Five have been given a 'retirement job', producing Henry the Green Engine for the Thomas the Tank Engine range.

As well as locomotives, super-detailing was extended to Hornby's new Pullman cars released in 2002. The set of five super-detailed Pullmans was produced with more surface and added-on detail than ever seen before in 00 scale, right down to table lamps with individual pinpoint lights. A preview in *Railway Modeller* announced that: 'In the field of passenger rolling stock, both loco-hauled and unitary, we find another example of all new tooling in the shape of a train of Pullman cars . . . these splendid vehicles will be based on the 1928-built MCW vehicles. They will feature a high level of detailing, including interiors, *lighting* and sprung buffers.'

During the late 1980s and early 1990s, particularly in the face of competition from Bachmann (from 1990), Hornby suffered from being labelled a toy manufacturer and therefore not a serious producer of accurate scale models.

The advent of super-detailed locomotives and rolling stock began to break down that barrier in the late 1990s but, as Simon Kohler points out, 'we're still having to work one hundred and ten per cent. We're having to work harder than the competition. It's about trying to break this toy image. Detail, detail, detail.' And this close attention to detail is having the desired effect. Justin Etkin points out that 'since they've moved production to China, Hornby have improved their quality greatly, and the collector is now coming into Hamleys for Hornby trains. Collectors who would have bought Bachmann before are now going back to Hornby.'

The move of production to China has been controversial, and has echoes of the arguments surrounding Meccano's adoption of plastic for rolling stock and some locomotives. But where Meccano refused to accept what market forces later showed to be an inevitable change, Hornby has embraced the challenge and moved remarkably quickly – and there is no doubt that the move to China is what has allowed Hornby to produce such finely detailed models and thereby

retain its reputation as Britain's leading model railway system. The super-detailed label was a conscious decision by Hornby to move forward and to reinforce the fact that the company was manufacturing model railways as opposed to toys. To quote Simon Kohler again, 'We were able to take some of our existing models and put more detail on them because they were made in China. We could do the valve gear, do the wheels, add separate rather than moulded detail, we could fine print. *That* was a super-detailed model.' Now that all of Hornby's models are manufactured in China with a similar attention to detail, the company is to drop the super-detailed label because from now on the description will apply to all of its models.

While all this detailing has been introduced at the top of the range, however Hornby has not forgotten its grass roots, and Simon Kohler tells the model railway press: 'Unless you get young people touching trains, model trains, toy trains, whatever, then our market will die out. Don't knock us for producing Thomas or Hogwarts. That's what gets people interested in model railways.'

It has been a long journey from the invention of Meccano during the reign of Queen Victoria, through the constructional toy trains of the 1920s, to the Chinese-made scale models of the 21st century. The models, the manufacturing and

the management may have changed but the attitude hasn't, and that is why the name Hornby is still the most respected in British model railways. In 1920, Meccano told its customers, 'We are very proud of this fine clockwork train system, and it will be a great favourite amongst boys', while dealers were informed that 'with the introduction of this line commences a new era in clockwork train construction'. In 2002, Simon Kohler says, 'We are proud of the fact that we produce excellent models which also make marvellous toys,' while the possibilities opened up by the move of production to China herald another new era in model train construction. One difference that has occurred in 80 years is that most of the people now using Hornby trains are adults. Many of them were introduced to model railways as children, and it is interesting to speculate what Hornby railways might have in store during the *next* 80 years for the children currently buying Thomas the Tank Engine and Hogwarts Express.

Below Further echoes of Dublo – the Class N2 tank was a founder member of the Hornby-Dublo system, and appeared in more variations than any other Dublo model. Hornby launched its ex-Airfix model of the N2 Tank in 2000, and this factory-weathered version was released in 2002.

i New Illustrated Encyclopaedia of Railways
ii Oxford Companion to British Railway History
iii British Railways' Steam Locomotive

HORNBY GAUGE O TRAIN

THE COMPLETENESS OF THE HORNBY GAUGE O RAILWAY SYSTEM

From the day of their introduction Hornby Trains have always represented the latest mo
Designs are continually being improved and new items added so that the system is con
every detail. There are Locomotives for all duties, driven by electric motors or by cl
Rolling Stock of all kinds, including Corridor Coaches, Pullman Cars, ordinary Coaches
for passenger services; and there are numerous and varied Wagons and Vans for frei

The Accessories are now better than ever before. Stations, Signals and Signal Cabins,
Crossings and other items can be obtained wired for electric lighting. Miniature Trees a
a splendid scenic setting for any layout; Tunnels add realism to the track; miniature
Passengers give "life" to station platforms; and there are Animals for lineside fields.

The splendid fun of running a Hornby Railway is real and lasting, because of the exce
reliability of Hornby Locomotives, the realistic appearance and easy running of the Ro
wide range of effective Accessories—all designed and built in proportion and all splend

HORNBY ELECTRIC AND CLOCKWORK LOCOMOTIVES

Hornby Electric Locomotives, of which there is a wide selection, are fitted with powerful
capable of hauling heavy loads at high speeds, but always under perfect control.
Locomotives can be controlled for speed, and for starting and stopping, from the lineside

Hornby Clockwork Locomotives are the longest-running locomotives of their resp
world. The motors are perfect mechanisms with accurately cut gears. All the locomot
either from the cab or from the track by means of a suitable brake rail.

THE FAMOUS HORNBY REMOTE CONTROL

The largest Hornby 20-volt Electric Locomotives are fitted with the famous Hornby Remote
possible starting and stopping; controlling for speed, easy round the curves, faster alon
reversing trains at the end of the run or when shunting, without any need to touch the
Everything is done from outside the track! In conjunction with the automatic coup
Rolling Stock, Remote Control makes possible the most realistic operation.

THE FINISH OF HORNBY LOCOMOTIVES

Hornby Locomotives are finished in the passenger traffic colours of the four Britis
red for L.M.S., light green for L.N.E.R., and dark green for G.W.R. and S.R. Locomotive
to special order finished in goods traffic colours—black for L.M.S., L.N.E.R. and S.R., and do

railway practice.
ete in practically
work.   There is
d Guard's Vans
working.

gine Sheds, Level
Hedging provide
ilway Staff and

nal strength and
Stock, and the
y finished.

d efficient motors
Hornby Electric

ve types in the
can be braked

trol. This makes
he straight; and
ocomotive at all.
gs fitted to the

Railway groups,
an be obtained
green for G.W.R.

Be Chief Engineer of your own Railway, like this boy!

Ready to give the "Right Away!"

Key dates

Opposite page Women hard at work on the production line in 1960.

Text in bold refers to Rovex events; text in plain refers to Meccano events.

9 January 1901
Patent granted for 'Mechanics Made Easy'

14 September 1907
Trade-name 'Meccano' registered

4 June 1908
Meccano Ltd is incorporated

July 1911
Patent granted for 'Raylo'

28 August 1914
Meccano Ltd moves to Binns Road factory

1915
'Raylo' introduced

1919
Lines Bros founded

1920
First Hornby train introduced
Tinprinted train introduced

1924
'Hornby Series' name adopted

1925
The electric Metropolitan train becomes available

1926
M Series introduced

1929
No 2 Specials introduced

21 September 1936
Frank Hornby dies

1937
'Princess Elizabeth' released

1938
Hornby-Dublo introduced

1939–1945
World War II

1946
Rovex Plastics founded

1948
'Duchess of Atholl' released

1950
First Rovex train set introduced

1951
Lines Bros buys Rovex Plastics

1952
Rovex Trains renamed Tri-ang Railways

1954
Rovex moves to Margate factory

1957
'Bristol Castle' released

1958
First diesel introduced to Dublo

1959
Dublo two-rail system introduced

1960
Ring Field Motor announced

14 February 1964
Lines Bros buys Meccano for £781,000

May 1965
Dublo 'amalgamated' with Tri-ang Railways to become Tri-ang Hornby

1966
Hornby-Dublo tools sold to G&R Wrenn Ltd

1969
Rovex Scale Models Ltd renamed Rovex-Tri-ang Ltd

28 May 1970
Meccano Ltd renamed
Meccano-Tri-ang Ltd

1971
Airfix Industries buys Meccano

1971
Lines Bros liquidated

1972
Rovex bought by DCM.
Tri-ang Hornby renamed
Hornby Railways

1976
Rovex Ltd renamed Hornby
Hobbies

1980
DCM liquidated

1981
Hornby Hobbies becomes an
independent company

1986
Hornby Group plc flotation

1994
G & R Wrenn Ltd sold to
Dapol Ltd

1995
First Hornby Railways model
to be made in China (Class 92
Electric)

1996
Hornby Railways renamed
Hornby
Hornby buys tools from
Dapol Ltd

1999
Last model made at Margate

UK catalogue locomotive types

This list is restricted to the date of introduction of each locomotive type, and does not include variations of power/control or the introduction of subsequent variations of livery or locomotive name/number except where models have been retooled. It does not include the 'Play' locomotives or the 'Transcontinental' locomotives produced with foreign markets in mind.

1920

Hornby Gauge 0

Locomotive for tinprinted train set (later renamed No 00 and later still M3 – first released as GNR/MR/LNWR 'George V')
Hornby tender locomotive '2710' (first released in black, green & red)

1921

Hornby Gauge 0

No 1 tender locomotive '2710' (improved Hornby locomotive – first released in black, green, red & blue)
No 2 tender locomotive '2711' (first released in red, green, black & blue)

1922

Hornby Gauge 0

Zulu tank locomotive (later renamed No 1 tank locomotive – first released in black only)
Zulu tender locomotive (later renamed No 0 locomotive – first released in black only)

1923

Hornby Gauge 0

Hornby tank locomotive (later renamed No 2 tank locomotive – first released in red, green & black)

1925

Hornby Gauge 0

Hornby electric locomotive (Metropolitan locomotive)

1926

Hornby Gauge 0

M Series locomotive (first released in green only)
Riviera Blue Train locomotive

1927

Hornby Gauge 0

No 3 tender locomotive (Royal Scot, Flying Scotsman, Caerphilly Castle and, in 1928, Lord Nelson)

Below Second series Suburban Station, first introduced to Tri-ang Railways in 1962.

1929

Hornby Gauge 0

No 1 Special tender locomotive (first released in all four company liveries)

No 1 Special tank locomotive (first released in all four company liveries)

No 2 Special tank locomotive (first released in all four company liveries)

No 2 Special tender locomotives:

LMS Compound '1185' (maroon)

LNER Shire class 'Yorkshire' (later issued as Hunt class '201 Bramham Moor' – both first released in green)

GWR Churchward County 'County of Bedford' (green)

SR Class L1 'A759' (green)

1930

Hornby Gauge 0

MO tender locomotive (later renamed No 20 - first released in green & red)

1931

Hornby Gauge 0

M3 tank locomotive (first released in all four company liveries)

1932

Hornby Gauge 0

'Swiss type' electric locomotive (with dummy pantographs)

'Continental' electric locomotive (modified Metropolitan locomotive)

1936

Hornby Gauge 0

No 0 'Silver Link' A4 class tender locomotive

1937

Hornby Gauge 0

No 4 'Eton' Schools class tender locomotive (first released in SR green and, extremely rare, SR black mainly for export)

'Princess Elizabeth' Princess Royal class tender locomotive (LMS maroon)

1938

Hornby-Dublo

0-6-2 tank locomotive, based on Class N2 and first released as:

LNER Class N2 Tank No 2690 (black)

SR Class E5 Tank No 2594 (green)

GWR standard Tank No 6699 (green)

Above The Hornby-Dublo Canadian Pacific locomotive, which was produced for export, was basically a 'Duchess' with a dummy headlight and a cowcatcher, while the caboose was adapted from the LMR brake van with the addition of a long chimney and a cupola.

Opposite page Recalling the pre-war tinplate tank wagons of the Gauge 0 system, in 1987 Hornby released one of its small tank wagons in the liveries of Redline and Castrol.

LMS Class 69 Tank No 6917 (black)

A4 class tender locomotive (first released as 'Sir Nigel Gresley' in LNER blue)

1939

Hornby-Dublo

'Duchess of Atholl' Princess Coronation class tender locomotive appeared in catalogues but was not available until after the war

1939-1945

World War II

1947

Hornby Gauge 0

No 101 tank locomotive (modified version of M3 tank, first released in all four company liveries – renamed No 40 in 1954 when first released in BR livery)

Hornby-Dublo

Princess Coronation (Duchess) class tender locomotive (first released as 'Duchess of Atholl' in LMS maroon)

1948

Hornby Gauge 0

No 501 tender locomotive (first released in all four company liveries – renamed No 50 and No 51 in 1954 when first released in BR black [50] and BR green [51])

1950

Rovex

Princess Royal class tender locomotive (first released as 'Princess Elizabeth')

1951

Tri-ang Railways

Class N2 tank locomotive

1952

Tri-ang Railways

Class 3F 'Jinty' tank locomotive

1954

Hornby-Dublo

Class 4MT standard tank locomotive

1956

Hornby Gauge 0

No 30 tender locomotive

Tri-ang Railways

Class 3 standard tank locomotive

0-6-0 Class 08 diesel shunter

Class S saddle tank locomotive

1957

Hornby-Dublo

Castle class tender locomotive (first released as 'Bristol Castle' in BR green)

Tri-ang Railways

Class 4SUB EMU

Dock Shunter 0-4-0 diesel shunter

1958

Hornby-Dublo

Class 8F tender locomotive

Bo-Bo diesel-electric locomotive

Tri-ang Railways

Class 101 DMU

Class 3F tender locomotive

1959

Hornby-Dublo

Class R1 tank locomotive

Tri-ang Railways

Steeple cab electric locomotive

1960

Hornby-Dublo

0-6-0 Class 08 diesel shunter

Co-Co 'Deltic' diesel-electric locomotive

Tri-ang Railways

Class L1 tender locomotive

'Britannia' class 7P6F tender locomotive

Industrial 0-4-0 tank locomotive

1961

Hornby-Dublo

Rebuilt West Country class tender locomotive
(first released as 'Barnstaple' in BR green)

Co-Bo diesel-electric locomotive

Tri-ang Railways

Dean Single tender locomotive

Class EM2 Co-Co electric locomotive

Battle of Britain/West Country class
tender locomotive

1962

Hornby-Dublo

Southern Region EMU/Electric Suburban Train

Tri-ang Railways

North British 0-4-0 diesel shunter

1963

Hornby-Dublo

0-4-0 tank locomotive of the starter sets

Tri-ang Railways

Class 31 A1A-A1A diesel locomotive

Class B12 tender locomotive

'Blue Pullman' DMU

Stephenson's 'Rocket'

Caledonian Single tender locomotive

1964

Hornby-Dublo

0-4-0 diesel shunter of the starter sets

E3000/Type AL1/Class 81 electric pantograph
locomotive (released as E3002)

1966

Tri-ang Hornby

Class 37/Type 3 Co-Co diesel-electric locomotive

E3000/Type AL1/Class 81 electric pantograph locomotive (released as E3001)

Hall class tender locomotive

1967

Tri-ang Hornby

Class 35 Hymek diesel hydraulic locomotive

Class M7 tank locomotive

Wrenn (using ex-Hornby-Dublo tools)

Castle class tender locomotive

Class 8F tender locomotive

Class 4MT tank locomotive

1968

Tri-ang Hornby

Class A1/A3 tender locomotive (first released as 'Flying Scotsman')

Wrenn (using ex-Hornby-Dublo tools)

Class R1 tank locomotive

Rebuilt West Country class tender locomotive

1969

Wrenn (using ex-Hornby-Dublo tools)

Class A4 tender locomotive

Princess Coronation (Duchess) class tender locomotive

0-6-2 tank locomotive based on Class N2

1970

Tri-ang Hornby

Princess Coronation class tender locomotive

1971

Tri-ang Hornby

Class 9F tender locomotive (first released as 'Evening Star')

Class 57XX pannier tank locomotive

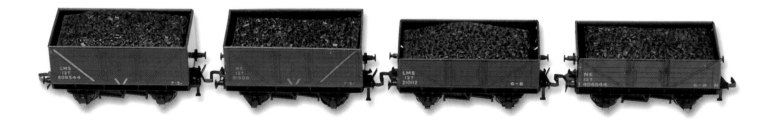

This page and opposite page A selection of the many and varied tinplate and die-cast Dublo goods wagons.

1973

Hornby Railways

Black Five class tender locomotive

Class 2P tender locomotive (modified from the Tri-ang Railways L1 first released in 1960)

1974

Wrenn (using ex-Hornby-Dublo tools)

0-6-0 Class 08 diesel shunter

1975

Hornby Railways

Class 47 Co-Co diesel-electric locomotive

Class 2 'Ivatt' tender locomotive

1976

Hornby Railways

Class J83 tank locomotive

Class N15 'King Arthur' tender locomotive

0-6-0 Class 08 diesel shunter (new body, Tri-ang version first introduced 1956)

1977

Hornby Railways

Princess Coronation (Duchess) class tender locomotive

Class 25 Bo-Bo diesel-electric locomotive

Class 43 'HST' (Inter-City 125)

Wrenn (using ex-Hornby-Dublo tools)

Bo-Bo diesel-electric locomotive

1978

Hornby Railways

Class 101 Holden tank locomotive

Class 29 Bo-Bo diesel-electric locomotive

King class (Class 6000) tender locomotive

Class 3F 'Jinty' tank locomotive (new body, originally introduced 1952)

1979

Hornby Railways

Class A4 tender locomotive (first released as 'Mallard')

Class E2 tank locomotive

Class 52 'Western' diesel hydraulic locomotive

Patriot class tender locomotive

1980

Hornby Railways

Class 0F 'Caledonian Pug' tank locomotive

Class 4P tank locomotive

Class B17/4 ('Footballer') tender locomotive (first released as 'Manchester United')

Class 370 APT (the 'tilting train')

King class tender locomotive retooled

1981, 'The Year of the Locomotive'

Hornby Railways

Class 2721 pannier tank locomotive Schools class tender locomotive (first released as 'Stowe')

Class 4P LMS Compound tender locomotive
(first released as No 1000)
Class D49/1 Shire/Hunt class tender locomotive
(first released as 'Cheshire')
Class 38XX Churchward County (first released
as 'County of Bedford')
Class J13/J52 saddle tank locomotive
Class 86/2 electric pantograph locomotive
A1/A3 class tender locomotive retooled
'Britannia' class tender locomotive partly
retooled

1982
Hornby Railways
Class 110 DMU
Class 58 diesel-electric locomotive

1984
Hornby Railways
Princess Royal class tender locomotive (first
released as 'The Princess Royal')

1986
Hornby Railways
Saint class tender locomotive

1987
Hornby Railways
Class 142 'Pacer' DMU
Class 06 0-4-0 diesel shunter

1988
Hornby Railways
Class 8F tender locomotive
Class 90 electric locomotive
Class 91 electric locomotive
1991

Hornby Railways
Class 2800 tender locomotive
Class D tank locomotive

1995
Hornby Railways
Class 92 electric locomotive (first released as
'Elgar')
Class 373 'Eurostar' (Jouef H0 scale model)

1996
Hornby Railways
Class 373 'Eurostar' (Hornby Railways 00
scale model)

1997
Hornby
Class 14XX tank locomotive
Castle class tender locomotive (first released as
'Winchester Castle')
Class 1000 Hawksworth County tender
locomotive
'Networker' DMU

1998
Hornby
'L&Y Pug' tank locomotive
Class A1X 'Terrier' tank locomotive
Class J94 'Austerity' saddle tank locomotive
Class 4F tender locomotive
Class 56 Co-Co diesel-electric locomotive
Class 2361 'Dean Goods' tender locomotive
A1/A3 class tender locomotive largely retooled
A4 class tender locomotive largely retooled

1999

Hornby

Class 2P tender locomotive (replaced 1973 version)

Class 155 Super Sprinter DMU

Class 61XX Prairie tank locomotive

9F class tender locomotive largely retooled

2000

Hornby

Class N2 tank locomotive

Princess Coronation class tender locomotive (first released as 'Duchess of Hamilton')

Rebuilt Merchant Navy class tender locomotive (first released as 'Clan Line')

Hornby Virtual Railway (HVR)

'Britannia' class tender locomotive largely retooled

2001

Hornby

Princess Coronation class tender locomotive (first released as 'Duchess of Hamilton')

Battle of Britain/West Country class tender locomotive (first released as 'Blackmoor Vale' and '92 Squadron' – replaced Tri-ang Railways

version introduced in 1961)

Princess Royal class tender locomotive (first released as 'Princess Arthur of Connaught' – replaced 1984 version)

2002

Hornby

Princess Coronation (Duchess) class tender locomotive (first released as 'Duchess of Rutland' and 'Duchess of Buccleuch' – replaced 1977 version)

Black Five tender locomotive (replaced 1973 version)

HVR-2

2003

Hornby

Information available at time of going to press:

Class 4P tank locomotive largely retooled

Class 8F tender locomotive largely retooled

King class tender locomotive retooled

Below Flying the flag – in 1992, Hornby started an annual tradition of releasing a 'Hornby' wagon carrying the company logo and the number of the year.

HORNBY

ELECTRIC AND CLOCKWORK

TRAIN

THE COMPLETENESS OF THE HORNBY RAILWAY SYSTEM

From the day of their introduction Hornby Trains have always represented the latest m
Designs are continually being improved and new items added so that the system is co
every detail. There are Locomotives for all duties, driven by electric motors or by c
Rolling Stock of all kinds, including Corridor Coaches, Pullman Cars, ordinary Coache
for passenger services; and there are numerous and varied Wagons and Vans for fre

The Accessories are now better than ever before. Stations, Signals and Signal Cabin
Crossings and other items can be obtained wired for electric lighting. Miniature Trees
a splendid scenic setting for any layout; Cuttings and Tunnels add realism to the trac
Staff and Passengers give "life" to station platforms; and there are Animals for linesi

The splendid fun of running a Hornby Railway is real and lasting, because of the exce
reliability of Hornby Locomotives, the realistic appearance and easy running of the Ro
wide range of effective Accessories—all designed and built in proportion and all spler

HORNBY ELECTRIC AND CLOCKWORK LOCOMOTIVES

Hornby Electric Locomotives, of which there is a wide selection, are fitted with powerfu
capable of hauling heavy loads at high speeds, but always under perfect control.
Locomotives can be controlled for speed, and for starting and stopping, from the lines

Hornby Clockwork Locomotives are the longest-running locomotives of their res
world. The motors are perfect mechanisms with accurately cut gears. All the locomo
either from the cab, or from the track by means of a suitable brake rail.

THE FAMOUS HORNBY REMOTE CONTROL

The latest Hornby 20-volt Electric Locomotives are fitted with the famous Hornby Remote
possible starting and stopping; controlling for speed, easy round the curves, faster alo
reversing trains at the end of the run or when shunting, without any need to touch th
Everything is done from outside the track! In conjunction with the automatic cou
Rolling Stock, Remote Control makes possible the most realistic operation.

THE FINISH OF HORNBY LOCOMOTIVES

Hornby Locomotives are finished in the passenger traffic colours of the four British railw
groups, red for L.M.S., light green for L.N.E.R., and dark green for G.W.R. and S.R. Loc
motives can be obtained to special order finished in goods traffic colours—black for L.M.
L.N.E.R. and S.R., and dark green for G.W.R.

S

railway practice.
lete in practically
work.   There is
nd Guard's Vans
working.

gine Sheds, Level
Hedging provide
iniature Railway
ields.

onal strength and
g Stock, and the
ly finished.

d efficient motors
Hornby Electric

ve types in the
s can be braked

ntrol. This makes
the straight; and
ocomotive at all.
gs fitted to the

Every Hornby Locomotive is
thoroughly tested and is
guaranteed to be in good
running order when it leaves our factory.
Hornby Trains are manufactured by Meccano
Limited, Liverpool, and are constructed
throughout by expert craftsmen from the
finest materials obtainable.

*Run your own Railway! The Hornby System
includes everything that is necessary to equip a
complete miniature railway, either electric or
clockwork, to be operated in exactly the same
way as a real railway system.*

Index

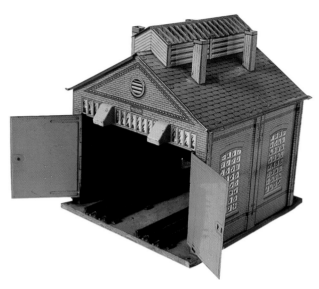

Above The Engine Shed was just one of the many impressive tinprinted buildings produced by Meccano – pictured is the E1E Engine Shed fitted with electric track and lighting.

Below Windsor Station, first introduced in 1923. It was an odd choice of name because in 1923 Hornby produced no trains in the liveries of the Great Western or Southern Railways, the two companies that operated stations in Windsor. The station was catalogued as the No 2 Station from 1928, with alternative names available from 1936. This version dates from 1934.

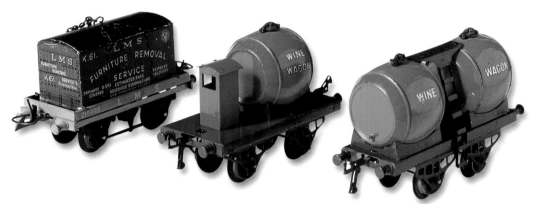

Left Single and Double Wine Wagons, and a Flat Truck loaded with an LMS furniture container.

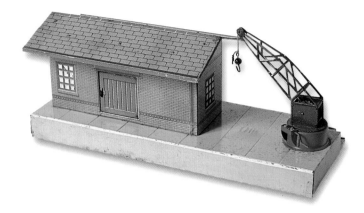

Below The popular Snowplough was first introduced in 1924, this Great Western version dating from 1926. The fan was operated by a drive belt connected to the front axle, which meant that in theory the snowplough could keep the tracks clear – unless, of course, it was the wrong kind of snow.

Bibliography

Below No other tank wagon looks like it or lasts like it… Since the days of Gauge 0, private owners' wagons and branded tank wagons had given Hornby the opportunity to introduce a number of colourful company logos to the system, but few were as striking as these two.

Beardsley, Roger, *The Hornby Companion* (New Cavendish Books, London, 1992)

Betts, C H & Watts, Matthias, *The Next War: The British Industries Fair* (Simpkin, Marshall, Hamilton, Kent & Co Ltd, London, 1916)

Casserley, H C (ed), *The Observer's Book of Railway Locomotives of Britain* (Frederick Warne & Co Ltd, London, 1960)

Cockman, F G, *British Railways' Steam Locomotives* (Shire Publications Ltd, Princes Risborough, 1998)

Foster, Michael, *Hornby Dublo Trains* (New Cavendish Books, London, 1980)

Gamble, Jim, *Frank Hornby – Notes and Pictures* (James G Gamble, Nottingham, 2001)

Gould, M P, *Frank Hornby, The Boy Who Made $1,000,000 With A Toy* (New Cavendish Books, London, 1975 [Originally published by Meccano Co Inc. New York, New York, 1915])

Graebe, Chris & Julie, *The Hornby Gauge 0 System* (New Cavendish Books, London, 1985)

Hammond, Pat, *The Story of Rovex, Volume 1: The Tri-ang Railways* (New Cavendish Books, London, 1993)

Hammond, Pat, *The Story of Rovex, Volume 2: Tri-ang Hornby* (New Cavendish Books, London, 1998)

Hammond, Pat, *The Story of Rovex, Volume 3: Hornby Railways* (New Cavendish Books, London, 2003)

Hammond, Pat (ed), *Ramsay's British Model Trains Catalogue* (Swapmeet Publications, Felixstowe, 2000)

Nock, O S, *Tri-ang Hornby Book of Trains* (Ian Allen, London)

Randall, Peter, *The Products of Binns Road* (New Cavendish Books, London, 1977)

Salisbury, David, *Toy Trains* (Shire Publications Ltd, Princes Risborough, 1994)

Simmons, Jack & Biddle, Gordon (eds), *The Oxford Companion to British Railway History* (OUP, Oxford, 1997)

Stevens-Stratten, S W (ed), *The Hornby Book of Trains 25-Year Edition* (Rovex Ltd, Kent, 1979)

Talbot, Patrick, 'Frank Hornby The Politician' (article), *Classic Toys Magazine* (Vol 1, Issue 1), 1994

Tufnell, Robert (ed), *The New Illustrated Railway Encyclopedia* (Chartwell Books, New Jersey, 2000

Acknowledgements

Ian Harrison would like to thank Pat Hammond, without whom this book could not have been written. The author would also like to thank the following people for giving of their time, energy, expertise and enthusiasm:

Caroline Allen

Phil Atkins and Lynne Thurston of the National Railway Museum

Roy Chambers

Justin Etkin of Hamleys

Chris Graebe

Norman Hatton of Hatton's of Liverpool

Mike King

Simon Kohler of Hornby

Richard Lines

Peter Oliver

Chris Reeve

David Shepherd

Veronica Sheppard of Pollock's Toy Museum

Peter Snow

Max Stafford-Clark

Dave Stone

Patrick Talbot

Alan Wells

Picture credits

Below In 1988, British Railways named a Class 86 electric locomotive in honour of Frank Hornby and, to coincide with the occasion, Hornby released a commemorative version of the Class 86 model, also carrying the name 'Frank Hornby'. Thirteen years later the nameplates of the real locomotive were presented to the Hornby Railway Collectors' Association.

From Hornby Archives

pages 2, 9, 11, 12, 14-15 (black and white images), 17, 21, 55, 125, 131, 136, 177, 189

From Pat Hammond

pages 7, 10, 14 (colour image), 16, 43, 54, 67, 70, 77, 80, 82, 84, 88 (top left hand corner), 92, 95 (top right hand corner), 97, 98, 101, 102, 112, 113, 114, 129, 139, 140, 141, 143, 151, 157 (top), 158, 162

All other photography by Colin Bowling for Essential Works.